The Faber Book of
NONSENSE VERSE

Books by Geoffrey Grigson

THE FABER BOOK OF POPULAR VERSE

THE FABER BOOK OF LOVE POEMS

THE FABER BOOK OF EPIGRAMS AND EPITAPHS

THE FABER BOOK OF POEMS AND PLACES

THE FIESTA AND OTHER POEMS
(Secker and Warburg)

THE GODDESS OF LOVE
(Constable)

THE CONTRARY VIEW
(Macmillan)

POEMS AND POETS
(Macmillan)

NOTES FROM AN ODD COUNTRY
(Macmillan)

DISCOVERIES OF BONES AND STONES
(Macmillan)

SAD DEATH OF AN IMPERIAL MONGOOSE
(Macmillan)

ANGLES AND CIRCLES AND OTHER POEMS
(Gollancz)

THE ENGLISHMAN'S FLORA
(Hart-Davis MacGibbon)

THE FABER BOOK OF
NONSENSE VERSE

with a sprinkling of
NONSENSE PROSE

chosen, with an introduction, by
GEOFFREY GRIGSON

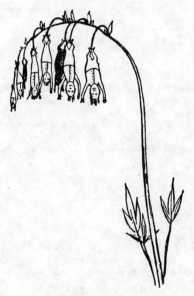

Manypeeplia Upsidownia

FABER AND FABER
LONDON   BOSTON

First published in 1979
by Faber and Faber Limited
3 Queen Square London WC1
First published in Faber Paperbacks 1982
Printed in Great Britain by
Fakenham Press Ltd, Fakenham, Norfolk
All rights reserved

Introduction and this selection
© 1979 Geoffrey Grigson

British Library Cataloguing in Publication Data

The Faber book of nonsense verse, with a sprinkling
of nonsense prose.
1. Nonsense-verses   2. English poetry
1. Grigson, Geoffrey
821'.07   PR1195.N/

ISBN 0-571-11356-7
ISBN 0-571-11787-2 Pbk

Divine Nonsensia, all thy sense infuse

JOHN HOOKHAM FRERE

Contents

Introduction

It wouldn't be sensible—in raising the curtain on a nonsense anthology—to be too serious or too historical about nonsense; or to say, with one's jaw stuck out, that proper word-nonsense is only of one kind or another. We see in front of us a poem. We prepare to read it in the poem way. It looks normal, the shape decidedly announces poem, it is divided into stanzas. We begin. The poem rhymes, it does no violence to syntax, and we discover that

> The common cormorant (or shag)
> Lays eggs inside a paper bag

or that a respectable elderly man in Spithead is opening his window (why not?), but calling out

> 'Fil-jomble, fil-jumble, Fil-rumble-comm-tumble.'

The poem attends inversely to natural history or human habits or human probabilities, and so on.

In nonsense-writing sense may suddenly give way to a nonsense chorus (the simple endearing trick of nursery rhymes). Nonsense adjectives, nouns, verbs, adverbs, animals, individuals, peoples, countries, are invented. Poems or prose (Rabelais, Thackeray, Lear, Christian Morgenstern) are even written in the writer's own useless Volapuk or Esperanto. And then nonsense poems can be situational rather than nonsensically verbal. Sense can underly nonsense. Nonsense can impart feeling. The many kinds of nonsense can be mixed in a single poem. Whatever the kind or the mixture, the nonsense poem—if it works—refreshes us by surprise, by invention, or by commenting, in what is said or how it is said, on sense taking itself too seriously or being pompous, or in fashion.

The moment literature develops, nonsense literature must be expected as both a counter-genre and an innocent game. So it begins often in parody. But if the parodist is an able poet nonsense in what he writes is likely to take over, and take off. Canning and his literary-political friends in their *Anti-Jacobin* began by parodying the pro-Jacobins and what looked to them like advanced or revolutionary sillybillyism, and then found that they were creating nonsense—years before the first inventions of Lear and Carroll—which had its own nonsensical independence.

A similar thing happened in Russia half a century later. In 1852, under the stifling Russian autocracy, the poet Alexei Konstantinovich Tolstoy and his two cousins invented their ridiculous bureacrat Koz'ma Prutkov: in Prutkov's poems, Prutkov's plays, Prutkov's Collected Works they parodied civil servants' conceit and self-satisfaction and pomposity; and they enjoyed doing it so much that the nonsense took over, surviving its time and the targets the trio had in front of them.

In England we have rather fancied ourselves as the pioneers and developers of nonsense writing. But then as well as Tolstoy in Russia (and later—see below—Daniil Kharms), think of the nonsense poems of Christian Morgenstern in Germany, and in France, long after Rabelais, of *Le Hareng Saur*, the Pickled Herring, of Charles Cros, which hung, *sec, sec, sec*, on the white wall, or the modern nonsense of Robert Desnos.

I doubt if any national literature in the world, once it is sure enough and conscious enough of itself, can fail to develop its nonsense writing, its nonsense verse in particular, doubly fathered by a sense of fun and a sense of the absurd. And remember what Charles Cros said in his *Hareng Saur* (page 224)

J'ai composé cette histoire,—simple, simple, simple,
Pour mettre en fureur les gens—graves, graves, graves,
Et amuser les enfants.

Poking fun and giving pleasure. But he wasn't quite telling the truth. I am sure he wrote of his herring as every poet writes: because certain words came to him, and nagged him till he lengthened them into a poem. Lewis Carroll, as everyone knows, was out for a walk in the country, on a hillside,* alone, on a bright

* I valued a fancy that Carroll might have been walking on Cumnor Hill above Oxford on that bright day, and that he might have run into serious

summer day, when there came into his head, for no discernible reason, the line 'For the Snark *was* a Boojum, you see.' Then later he completed a single stanza, incorporating that *donnée*, from which grew, or to which he added another 140 stanzas, to complete *The Hunting of the Snark*.

Nonsense poetry, at its best, at its least contaminated, leaves parody, leaves satire, leaves the literature against which it is set, for its own freedom; and, as in all literature, there is the customary difference between good nonsense and cheap nonsense, which will explain certain absences in this anthology. (Think of that before you say 'But he has left this out, he has left that out': nonsense is not to be written for a living, like leading articles, or to a programme. As Dwight MacDonald remarked of parodists in his excellent book on parody, among nonsense writers there is a tendency to philistinism, especially among recent ones, though it began strongly with W. S. Gilbert and with imitators of Lewis Carroll.)

As for its nature, I see in nonsense poems, in words and situations, an inconsequent, sophisticated and good humoured playing; I see in nonsense poems a special kind of liberated 'mirth', much as John de Trevisa, 500 years ago, wrote of animals that 'Some beestis servythe for mannys myrth: as apes and murmusettes and popyngayes.' You cannot but see something of the nature of nonsense verse in the nature, shapes and names of its special fauna, oyster, lobster, herring, red herring, pickled herring, owl, pelican, snail, crocodile, kangaroo, dormouse, walrus, llama, et cetera.

Nonsense, in our special sense, has not much to do, I would say, with the rather boring, institutionalized, demodé and now academically studied nonsense of surrealism, which conformed too much to a conscious theory, to a programme; and I wouldn't be happy about much of a shift to a black nonsense, such as informed the extraordinary 'mini-stories' (page 296) of Daniil

Matthew Arnold with serious non-nonsensical words coming into *his* head and demanding a poem. And I thought of them crossing together in the punt at Bablocke Hythe, arms round each other, in token that poetry is a union of sense and nonsense. But no, Carroll was walking outside Guildford.

Kharms, melancholic poet lost under the weight of the Russian Revolution, who so much admired Edward Lear, was a friend of Malevich the painter, and kept in his Leningrad room 'a machine for doing nothing', made up of empty cigarette boxes, springs, tins, bicycle wheels and pieces of string.* Into black nonsense of his kind creeps a design on the reader; whereas the better non-sensifiers from Bishop Corbet downwards are happy in a corner juggling with their words, and released, for that while, from their melancholy.

Free as it may be (could anything be more free than a perfect, complex spoonerism?), the best nonsense verse—the writing of it certainly—is in danger now because it does demand an accepted idea of the nature of verse in general, a widely shared idea of the ways in which poetry works. Against accepted forms and poetic tricks and poetry language, it plays its own nature and language. Edward Lear, that melancholic, intelligent genius of a poet, needed Tennyson to play against, for instance, although Lear's

> Spoonmeat at Bill Porter's in the Hall

or Lear's

> Cold are the crabs that crawl on yonder hills,
> Colder the cucumbers that grow beneath

are still the man, the nonsense poet, in his own liberty.

I suppose that nonsense set going by writing which is formless and anarchic won't be much fun. For future nonsense verse which is deeply mirthful we may have to wait, whenever it comes, in whatever shape, for a reasserted common art which is deeply artful. As for now—hence this anthology—we still have in our heads enough of the older forms of verse to enjoy the older nonsense.

But this is getting too serious. When Maria Edgeworth lifted Samuel Foote's famous nonsense mnemonic (page 59) about the great she-bear and the Picninnies and the Joblillies and the

---

* I owe a knowledge of these Russian nonsense poets to Robin Milner-Gulland, Reader in Russian at Sussex University.

Garyulies and put it into a chapter of didactic educational fiction, she made the father remark, as the children tried to repeat it without mistake, that 'It is sweet to talk nonsense in season.'

Good advice, and true. And enough.

GEOFFREY GRIGSON

Mannerly Margery Milk and Ale

Ay, beshrew you! by my fay,
These wanton clerks be nice alway!
Avaunt, avaunt, my popinjay!
What, will ye do nothing but play?
Tilly vally, straw, let be I say!
Gup, Christian Clout, gup, Jack of the Vale!
With Mannerly Margery Milk and Ale.

By God, ye be a pretty pode,
And I love you an whole cart-load.
Straw, James Foder, ye play the fode,
I am no hackney for your rod:
Go watch a bull, your back is broad!
Gup, Christian Clout, gup, Jack of the Vale!
With Mannerly Margery Milk and Ale.

Ywis ye deal uncourteously;
What, would ye frumple me? now fy!
What, and ye shall be my pigesnye?
By Christ, ye shall not, no hardely;
I will not be japéd bodily!
Gup, Christian Clout, gup, Jack of the Vale!
With Mannerly Margery Milk and Ale.

Walk forth your way, ye cost me nought;
Now have I found that I have sought:
The best cheap flesh that ever I bought.
Yet, for His love that all hath wrought,
Wed me, or else I die for thought.
Gup, Christian Clout, you breath is stale!

Go, Mannerly Margery Milk and Ale!
Gup, Christian Clout, gup, Jack of the Vale!
With Mannerly Margery Milk and Ale.

JOHN SKELTON

My heart of gold as true as steel,
    As I me leanéd to a bough,
In faith but if ye love me well,
    Lord, so Robin lough!

My lady went to Canterbury,
    The saint to be her boot;
She met with Kate of Malmesbury:
    Why sleepest thou in an apple root?

Nine mile to Michaelmas,
    Our dame began to brew;
Michael set his mare to grass,
    Lord, so fast it snew!

For you, love, I brake my glass,
    Your gown is furred with blue;
The 'devil is dead, for there I was;
    Iwis it is full true.

And if ye sleep, the cock will crow,
    True heart, think what I say;
Jackanapes will make a mow,
    Look, who dare say him nay?

I pray you have me now in mind,
    I tell you of the matter;
He blew his horn against the wind;
    The crow goeth to the water.

Yet I tell you mickle more;
   The cat lieth in the cradle;
I pray you keep true heart in store;
   A penny for a ladle.

I swear by Saint Katharine of Kent,
   The goose goeth to the green;
All our dogges tail is brent,
   It is not as I ween.

Tirlery lorpin, the laverock sang,
   So merrily pipes the sparrow,
The cow brake loose, the rope ran home,
   Sir, God give you good-morrow!

ANON
early sixteenth century

[Shrovetide's Countenance]

'Tis a wonderful thing, continued Xenomanes, to hear and see
the state of Shrovetide.

If he chanced to spit, it was whole basketsful of goldfinches.
If he blowed his nose, it was pickled grigs.
When he wept, it was ducks with onion sauce.
When he sneezed, it was whole tubfuls of mustard.
When he coughed, it was boxes of marmalade.
When he sobbed, it was watercresses.
When he yawned, it was potfuls of pickled peas.
When he sighed, it was dried neats' tongues.
When he whistled, it was a whole scuttleful of green apes.
When he snored, it was a whole panful of fried beans.
When he frowned, it was soused hogs' feet.
When he spoke, it was coarse brown russet cloth; so little it

was like crimson silk, with which Parisatis desired that the words of such as spoke to her son Cyrus, King of Persia, should be interwoven.

When he blowed, it was indulgence money-boxes.
When he winked, it was buttered buns.
When he grumbled, it was March cats.
When he nodded, it was ironbound waggons.
When he made mouths, it was broken staves.
When he trembled, it was large venison pasties.
When he did sweat, it was old ling with butter sauce.
When he belched, it was bushels of oysters.
When he muttered, it was lawyers' revels.
When he hopped about, it was letters of licence and protections.
When he stepped back, it was sea cockle-shells.
When he slabbered, it was common ovens.
When he was hoarse, it was an entry of morrice-dancers.
When he broke wind, it was dun cows' leather spatterdashes.
When he funked, it was washed-leather boots.
When he scratched himself, it was new proclamations.
When he sung, it was peas in cods.
When he evacuated, it was mushrooms and morilles.
When he puffed, it was cabbages with oil, alias caules amb'olif.
When he talked, it was the last year's snow.
When he dreamt, it was of a cock and a bull.
When he gave nothing, so much for the bearer.
If he thought to himself, it was whimsies and maggots.
If he dozed, it was leases of lands.

FRANÇOIS RABELAIS
(tr. Sir Thomas Urquhart)

I will have the Whetstone

Hey, hey, hey, hey,
I will have the whetstone and I may.

I saw a dog seething souse
And an ape thatching an house
And a pudding eating a mouse.
I will have the whetstone and I may.

I saw an urchin shape and sewe
And anoder bake and brew,
Scour the pots as they were new.
I will have the whetstone and I may.

I saw a codfish corn sow,
And a worm a whistle blow
And a pye treading a crow.
I will have the whetstone and I may.

I saw a stockfish drawing a harrow
And anoder driving a barrow
And a saltfish shooting an arrow.
I will have the whetstone and I may.

I saw a boar burdens bind
And a frog clewens wind
And a toad mustard grind.
I will have the whetstone and I may.

I saw a sow bear kyrchers to wash,
The second sow had an hedge to plash,
The third sow went to the barn to thrash.
I will have the whetstone and I may.

I saw an egg eating a pie,
Geven me drink, my mouth is dry,
It is not long sith I made a lie.
I will have the whetstone and I may.

ANON
sixteenth century

21

The white dove sat on the castle wall,
I bend my bow and shoot her I shall,
I put her in my glove both feathers and all;
I laid my bridle upon the shelf,
If you will any more, sing it yourself.

W. WAGER

A Tetrastich in the Lanternish Language

Briszmarg dalgotbrick nubstzne zos,
Isquebsz prusq: albok crinqs zacbac.
Mizbe dilbarskz morp nipp stancz bos,
Strombtz, Panurge, walmap quost gruszbac.

FRANÇOIS RABELAIS

The Three Wise Men of Gotham

There were three men of Gotham,
   As I have heard men say,
That needs would ride a hunting
   Upon Saint David's day.

All the day they hunted,
   And nothing could they find
But a ship a-sailing,
   A-sailing with the wind.

One said it was a ship,
   The other he said, nay;
The third said it was a house,
   With the chimney blown away.

And all the night they hunted,
   And nothing could they find
But the moon a-gliding,
   A-gliding with the wind.

One said it was the moon,
   The other he said, nay;
The third said it was a cheese,
   And half o't cut away.

And all the day they hunted,
   And nothing could they find
But a hedgehog in a bramble bush,
   And that they left behind.

The first said it was a hedgehog,
   The second he said, nay;
The third it was a pincushion,
   And the pins stuck in wrong way.

And all the night they hunted,
   And nothing could they find
But a hare in a turnip field,
   And that they left behind.

The first said it was a hare,
   The second he said, nay;
The third said it was a calf,
   And the cow had run away.

And all the day they hunted,
   And nothing could they find
But an owl in a holly tree,
   And that they left behind.

One said it was an owl,
   The other he said, nay,
The third said 'twas an old man,
   And his beard growing grey.

ANON

The Author Loving these Homely Meats Specially, viz.: Cream, Pancakes, Buttered Pippin-pies (Laugh, Good People) and Tobacco; Writ to that Worthy and Virtuous Gentlewoman, whom He Calleth Mistress, as Followeth

If there were, oh! an Hellespont of cream
Between us, milk-white mistress, I would swim
To you, to show to both my love's extreme,
Leander-like,—yea! dive from brim to brim.
But met I with a buttered pippin-pie
Floating upon 't, that would I make my boat
To waft me to you without jeopardy,
Though sea-sick I might be while it did float.
Yet if a storm should rise, by night or day,
Of sugar-snows and hail of caraways,
Then, if I found a pancake in my way,
It like a plank should bring me to your kays;
   Which having found, if they tobacco kept,
   The smoke should dry me well before I slept.

JOHN DAVIES OF HEREFORD

Sir Eglamour

Sir Eglamour, that worthy knight,
He took his sword and went to fight;
And as he rode both hill and dale,
Armëd upon his shirt of mail,
A dragon came out of his den,
Had slain, God knows how many men!

When he espied Sir Eglamour,
Oh, if you had but heard him roar,
And seen how all the trees did shake,
The knight did tremble, horse did quake,
The birds betake them all to peeping—
It would have made you fall a weeping!

But now it is vain to fear,
Being come unto, 'fight dog! fight bear!'
To it they go and fiercely fight
A live-long day from morn till night.
The dragon had a plaguy hide,
And could the sharpest steel abide.

No sword will enter him with cuts,
Which vexed the knight unto the guts;
But, as in choler he did burn,
He watched the dragon a good turn;
And, as a yawning he did fall,
He thrust his sword in, hilts and all.

Then, like a coward, he did fly
Unto his den that was hard by;
And there he lay all night and roared.
The knight was sorry for his sword,
But, riding thence, said, 'I forsake it,
He that will fetch it, let him take it!'

SAMUEL ROWLANDS

Mockado, Fustian, and Motley

Sweet semi-circled Cynthia played at maw,
The whilst Endymion ran the wild-goose chase:
Great Bacchus with his cross-bow killed a daw,
And sullen Saturn smiled with pleasant face:
The ninefold Bugbears of the Caspian lake
Sat whistling ebon hornpipes to their ducks;
Madge-owlet straight for joy her girdle brake,
And rugged Satyrs frisked like stags and bucks:
The untamed tumbling fifteen-footed Goat
With promulgation of the Lesbian shores
Confronted Hydra in a sculler boat,
At which the mighty mountain Taurus roars:
    Meantime great Sultan Soliman was born,
    And Atlas blew his rustic rumbling horn.

JOHN TAYLOR

The Satyrs' Catch

Buzz, quoth the blue fly,
    Hum, quoth the bee:
Buzz and hum, they cry,
    And so do we.
In his ear, in his nose,
    Thus, do you see?
He ate the dormouse,
    Else it was he.

BEN JONSON

Ha ha! ha! ha! This world doth pass
   Most merrily I'll be sworn,
For many an honest Indian ass
   Goes for a unicorn.
               Fara diddle dyno,
               This is idle fyno.

Tie hie! tie hie! O sweet delight!
   He tickles this age that can
Call Tullia's ape a marmasyte
   And Leda's goose a swan.
               Fara diddle dyno,
               This is idle fyno.

So so! so so! Fine English days!
   For false play is no reproach,
For he that doth the coachman praise
   May safely use the coach.
               Fara diddle dyno,
               This is idle fyno.

ANON: 1608

Martin said to his man
   Fie man, fie!
O Martin said to his man
   Who's the fool now?
Martin said to his man
Fill thou the cup and I the can,
Thou hast well drunken, man,
   Who's the fool now?

I see a sheep shearing corn.
   Fie man, fie!
I see a sheep shearing corn.
   Who's the fool now?

I see a sheep shearing corn,
And a cuckold blow his horn.
Thou hast well drunken, man,
   Who's the fool now?

I see a man in the moon.
   Fie man, fie!
I see a man in the moon.
   Who's the fool now?
I see a man in the moon
Clouting of Saint Peter's shoon.
Thou hast well drunken, man,
   Who's the fool now?

I see a hare chase a hound.
   Fie man, fie!
I see a hare chase a hound.
   Who's the fool now?
I see a hare chase a hound
Twenty mile above the ground.
Thou hast well drunken, man,
   Who's the fool now?
I see a goose ring a hog.
   Fie man, fie!

I see a goose ring a hog.
   Who's the fool now?
I see a goose ring a hog,
And a snail that did bite a dog.
Thou hast well drunken, man,
   Who's the fool now?
I see a mouse catch the cat.
   Fie man, fie!

I see a mouse catch the cat.
   Who's the fool now?

I see a mouse catch the cat
And the cheese to eat the rat.
Thou hast well drunken, man,
    Who's the fool now?

            ANON: 1609

Ut, re, mi, fa, sol, la,
La, sol, fa, mi, re, ut.
    Hey down a down a!

My heart of gold, as true as steel,
    As I me leant unto the bowers,
But if my lady love me well,
    Lord, so Robin lowers.

      Heave and ho,
      Rumbelo.
    Hey trolo, troly lo!

My lady's gone to Canterbury,
    Saint Thomas, be her boot!
She met with Kate of Malmesbury,
    Why weep'st thou, maple root?

O sleep'st thou or wak'st thou, Jeffery Cook?
The roast it burns; turn round about.

    O Friar, how fares thy bandelow?
    Friar, how fares thy sandelow?

            ANON: 1609

Ut, re, mi, fa, mi, re, ut.
　　Hey derry derry,
　　Sing and be merry,
　　　Quando veni,
　　　Quando coeli,
Whip little David's bum.

ANON: 1609

A Non Sequitor

Mark how the lanterns cloud mine eyes!
See where a moon-drake gins to rise!
Saturn crawls much like an iron cat
To see the named moon in a slipshoed hat.
　　Thunder-thumping toadstools crock the pots
　　　To see the mermaids tumble;
　　Leather cat-a-mountains shake their heels
　　　To hear the goshawk grumble.
　　　　The rustic threed
　　　　Begins to bleed,
　　　　And cobwebs' elbows itches;
　　　　The putrid skies
　　　　Eat mulsack pies,
　　　　Backed up in logic breeches.

Monday trenchers make good hay,
　　The lobster wears no dagger;
Meal-mouth'd she-peacocks powl the stars,
　　And make the lowbell stagger.
　　　Blue crocodiles foam in the toe,
　　　Blind meal-bags do follow the doe;
　　　A rib of apple-brain spice

Will follow the Lancashire dice.
Hark, how the chime of Pluto's pisspot cracks,
To see the rainbow's wheel ganne, made of flax.

RICHARD CORBETT

Nonsense

Like to the thund'ring tone of unspoke speeches,
Or like a lobster clad in logic breeches,
Or like the gray frieze of a crimson cat,
Or like a moon-calf in a slipshoo hat,
Or like a shadow when the sun is gone,
Or like a thought that ne'er was thought upon,
 Even such is man, who never was begotten
 Until his children were both dead and rotten.

Like to the fiery touchstone of a cabbage,
Or like a crablouse with his bag and baggage,
Or like th'abortive issue of a a fizzle,
Or like the bag-pudding of a plowman's whistle,
Or like the four-square circle of a ring,
Or like the singing of hey down a ding,
 Even such is man, who, breathless without doubt,
 Spake to small purpose when his tongue was out.

Like to the green fresh fading withered rose,
Or like to rhyme or verse that runs in prose,
Or like the humbles of a tinder-box,
Or like a man that's sound, yet hath the pox,
Or like a hobnail coin'd in single pence,
Or like the present preterperfect tense,
 Even such is man, who died and then did laugh
 To see such strange lines writ on's epitaph.

RICHARD CORBETT

31

A Copy of Non Sequitors

Great Jack of Lent, clad in a robe of air,
Threw mountains higher than Alcides' beard:
Whilst Pancras Church, arm'd with a sapphire blade,
Began to reason on the business thus:
Ye squand'ring Troglodites of Amsterdam,
How long shall Cerberus a tapster be?
What if stout Ajax lay with Proserpine,
Must men leave eating powder'd beef for that?
For in the Commentaries of Tower Ditch
A fat stew'd bawd hath been a dish of state.
Will you forbid a man to pick his teeth,
Cause Brutus with a sword did slay himself?
Or if an humble bee do kill a whale,
With the butt end of the antarctic pole?
Why these are not the things at which we aim:
More might be said, but then more must be spoke,
The weights fell down because the jackrope broke.
    And he that of these verses maketh doubt,
    Let him sit down and pick the meaning out.

ANON: C. 1630

If all the World were Paper

If all the world were paper,
    And all the sea were ink,
If all the trees were bread and cheese,
    How should we do for drink?

If all the world were sand O,
    Oh then what should we lack O,
If as they say there were no clay,
    How should we take tobacco?

If all our vessels ran-a,
　　If none but had a crack-a,
If Spanish apes ate all the grapes,
　　How should we do for sack-a?

If all the world were men,
　　And men lived all in trenches,
And there were none but we alone,
　　How should we do for wenches?

If friars had no bald pates,
　　Nor nuns had no dark cloisters,
If all the seas were beans and peas,
　　How should we do for oysters?

If there had been no projects,
　　Nor none that did great wrongs,
If fiddlers shall turn players all,
　　How should we do for songs?

If all things were eternal,
　　And nothing their end bringing,
If this should be, then how should we
　　Here make an end of singing?

ANON

The Man in the Wilderness

The man in the wilderness asked of me,
How many strawberries grew in the sea?
I answered him as I thought good
As many red herrings as grew in a wood.

ANON: 1641

Nonsense

Oh that my lungs could bleat like butter'd pease;
But bleating of my lungs hath caught the itch,
And are as mangy as the Irish Seas,
That doth ingender windmills on a bitch.

I grant that rainbows, being lull'd asleep,
Snort like a woodknife in a lady's eyes;
Which makes her grieve to see a pudding creep,
For creeping puddings only please the wise.

Not that a hard roed herring should presume
To swing a tithe pig in a catskin purse;
For fear the hailstones which did fall at Rome,
By less'ning of the fault should make it worse.

For 'tis most certain winter woolsacks grow
From geese to swans, if men should keep them so,
Till that the sheep shorn planets gave the hint,
To pickle pancakes in Geneva print.

Some men there were that did suppose the sky
Was made of carbonado'd antidotes;
But my opinion is, a whale's left eye
Need not be coined all King Harry groats.

The reason's plain, for Charon's western barge
Running a tilt at the subjunctive mood,
Beckoned to Bednal Green, and gave him charge
To fasten padlocks with antarctic food.

The end will be the millponds must be laded,
To fish for white-pots in a country dance;
So they that suffered wrong and were upbraided
Shall be made friends in a left handed trance.

ANON: C. 1655

34

A Fancy

When Piecrust first began to reign,
  Cheese-parings went to war,
Red Herrings lookt both blue and wan,
  Green Leeks and Puddings jar.
Blind Hugh went out to see
  Two cripples run a race,
The Ox fought with the Humble Bee
  And claw'd him by the face.

ANON: 1656

Three Blind Mice

Three blind Mice, three blind Mice,
Dame Julian, Dame Julian,
The Miller and his merry old wife,
She scrap'd her tripe, lick thou the knife.

ANON: 1656

Ad Johannuelem Leporem, Lepidissimum, Carmen Heroicum

I sing the furious battles of the Spheres
Acted in eight and twenty fathom deep,
And from that time, reckon so many years
You'll find Endymion fell fast asleep.

And now assist me, O ye Musiques nine
That tell the orbs in order as they fight,
And thou, dread Atlas, with thine eyes so fine
Smile on me now that first began to write.

Pompey that once was tapster of New June,
And fought with Caesar on th' Aemathian plains,
First with his dreadful Myrmidons came in,
And let them blood in the hepatic veins.

But then an antelope in sable blue,
Clad like the Prince of Aurange in his cloak,
Studded with satires, on his army drew,
And presently Pheander's army broke.

Philip for hardiness surnamed Chubb,
In beauty equal to fork bearing Bacchus,
Made such a thrust at Phoebe with his club,
That made the Parthians cry, She will becack us;

Which heard, the Delphic Oracle drew nigh
To wipe fair Phoebe, if aught were amiss,
But Heliotrope, a little crafty spy,
Cried clouts were needless, for she did but piss.

A subtle glow-worm lying in a hedge,
And heard the story of sweet cheek'd Apollo,
Snatch'd from bright Stryopes his antic sledge,
And to the butter'd flounders cried out Holla.

Holla, you pamper'd jades, quoth he, look here;
And mounting straight upon a lobster's thigh,
An Englishman inflam'd with double beer,
Swore never to drink to man, a woman by.

By this time grew the conflict to be hot,
Boots against boots, 'gainst sandals, sandals fly,
Many poor thirsty men went to the pot,
Feathers lopped off, spurs everywhere did lie.

Cetera desiderantur.

ANON: 1658

When a Twister, a-twisting, will twist him a twist;
For the twisting of his twist, he three times doth intwist;
But, if one of the twines of the twist do untwist,
The twine that untwisteth, untwisteth the twist.

JOHN WALLIS
(from the French)

from *The Vision of Mac Conglinne*

A vision that appeared to me,
An apparition wonderful
    I tell to all:
There was a coracle all of lard
Within a port of New-milk Lake
    Upon the world's smooth sea.

We went into that man-of-war,
'Twas warrior-like to take the road
    O'er ocean's heaving waves.
Our oar-strokes then we pulled
Across the level of the main,
Throwing the sea's harvest up
    Like honey, the sea-soil.

The fort we reached was beautiful,
With works of custards thick,
    Beyond the lake.
Fresh butter was the bridge in front,
The rubble dyke was fair white wheat,
    Bacon the palisade.

Stately, pleasantly it sat,
A compact house and strong.
    Then I went in:

The door of it was hung beef,
The threshold was dry bread,
    Cheese-curds the walls.

Smooth pillars of old cheese
And sappy bacon props
    Alternate ranged;
Stately beams of mellow cream,
White posts of real curds
    Kept up the house.

Behind it was a well of wine,
Beer and bragget in streams,
    Each full pool to the taste.
Malt in smooth wavy sea
Over a lard-spring's brink
    Flowed through the floor.

A lake of juicy pottage
Under a cream of oozy lard
    Lay 'twixt it and the sea.
Hedges of butter fenced it round,
Under a crest of white-mantled lard
    Around the wall outside.

A row of fragrant apple-trees,
An orchard in its pink-tipped bloom,
    Between it and the hill.
A forest tall of real leeks,
Of onions and of carrots, stood
    Behind the house.

Within, a household generous,
A welcome of red, firm-fed men,
    Around the fire:
Seven bead-strings and necklets seven
Of cheeses and of bits of tripe
    Round each man's neck.

The Chief in cloak of beefy fat
Beside his noble wife and fair
    I then beheld.
Below the lofty caldron's spit
Then the Dispenser I beheld,
    His fleshfork on his back.

Wheatlet son of Milklet,
Son of juicy Bacon,
    Is mine own name.
Honeyed Butter-roll
Is the man's name
    That bears my bag.

Haunch of Mutton
Is my dog's name,
    Of lovely leaps.
Lard, my wife,
Sweetly smiles
    Across the brose.

Cheese-curds, my daughter,
Goes round the spit,
    Fair is her fame.
Corned Beef is my son,
Who beams over a cloak,
    Enormous, of fat.

Savour of Savours
Is the name of my wife's maid:
Morning-early
Across New-milk Lake she went.

Beef-lard, my steed,
An excellent stallion
    That increases studs;

A guard against toil
Is the saddle of cheese
    Upon his back.

A large necklace of delicious cheese-curds
    Around his back;
His halter and his traces all
    Of fresh butter.

(tr. Kuno Meyer) from the twelfth-century Irish

An Invitation to Lubberland

There's all sorts of fowl and fish,
    With wine and store of brandy,
Ye have there what your hearts can wish,
    The hills are sugar candy.

There is a ship we understand
    Now riding in the river,
'Tis newly come from Lubberland,
    The like I think was never;
You that a lazy life do love,
    I'd have you now go over,
They say land is not above
    Two thousand leagues from Dover.

The Captain and the Master too
    Do's give us this relation,
And so do's all the whole ship's crew,
    Concerning this strange nation.
The streets are pav'd with pudding-pies,
    Nay powder'd beef and bacon,
They say they scorn to tell you lies,
    Who think it is mistaken.

The king of knaves and queen of sluts
    Reign there in peace and quiet;
You need not fear to starve your guts,
    There is such store of diet:
There you may live free from all care,
    Like hogs set up a fatning,
The garments which the people wear
    Is silver, silk and sattin.

The lofty buildings of this place
    For many years have lasted,
With nutmegs, pepper, cloves and mace
    The walls are roughly casted,
In curious hasty-pudding boil'd,
    And most ingenious carving.
Likewise they are with pancakes ty'd,
    Sure, here's no fear of starving.

The Captain says, in every town
    Hot roasted pigs will meet ye,
They in the streets run up and down,
    Still crying out, come eat me:
Likewise he says, at every feast
    The very fowls and fishes,
Nay, from the biggest to the least,
    Comes tumbling to the dishes.

The rivers run with claret fine,
    The brooks with rich Canary,
The ponds with other sorts of wine,
    To make your hearts full merry:
Nay, more than this, you may behold
    The fountains flow with brandy,
The rocks are like refined gold,
    The hills are sugar candy.

Rosewater is the rain they have
    Which comes in pleasant showers,
All places are adorned brave
    With sweet and fragrant flowers;
Hot custards grow on ev'ry tree,
    Each ditch affords rich jellies.
Now, if you will be rul'd by me,
    Go there, and fill your bellies.

There's nothing there but holy-days,
    With musick out of measure;
Who can forbear to speak the praise
    Of such a land of pleasure?
There you may lead a lazy life,
    Free from all kinds of labour,
And he that is without a wife,
    May borrow of his neighbour.

There is no law, nor lawyers fees,
    All men are free from fury,
For ev'ry one do's what he please,
    Without a judge or jury:
The summer-time is warm they say,
    The winter's ne'er the colder,
They have no landlord's rent to pay,
    Each man is a free-holder.

You that are free to cross the seas,
    Make no more disputation,
At Lubberland you'll live at ease,
    With pleasant recreation:
The captain waits but for a gale,
    Of prosperous wind and weather,
And that they soon will hoist up sail,
    Make haste away together.

                                    ANON

Peter Piper picked a peck of pickled pepper
    Off a pewter plate;
A peck of pickled pepper Peter Piper picked
    Off a pewter plate;
If Peter Piper picked a peck of pickled pepper
    Off a pewter plate,
Where's the peck of pickled pepper Peter Piper picked
    Off a pewter plate?

ANON

Brian O'Linn

Brian O'Linn was a gentleman born,
His hair it was long and his beard unshorn,
His teeth were out and his eyes far in—
'I'm a wonderful beauty,' says Brian O'Linn!

Brian O'Linn was hard up for a coat,
He borrowed the skin of a neighbouring goat,
He buckled the horns right under his chin—
'They'll answer for pistols,' says Brian O'Linn!

Brian O'Linn had no breeches to wear,
He got him a sheepskin to make him a pair,
With the fleshy side out and the woolly side in—
'They are pleasant and cool,' says Brian O'Linn!

Brian O'Linn had no hat to his head,
He stuck on a pot that was under the shed,
He murdered a cod for the sake of his fin—
''Twill pass for a feather,' says Brian O'Linn!

Brian O'Linn had no shirt to his back,
He went to a neighbour and borrowed a sack.
He puckered a meal-bag under his chin—
'They'll take it for ruffles,' says Brian O'Linn!

Brian O'Linn had no shoes at all,
He bought an old pair at a cobbler's stall,
The uppers were broke and the soles were thin—
'They'll do me for dancing,' says Brian O'Linn!

Brian O'Linn had no watch for to wear,
He bought a fine turnip and scooped it out fair,
He slipped a live cricket right under the skin—
'They'll think it is ticking,' says Brian O'Linn!

Brian O'Linn was in want of a brooch,
He stuck a brass pin in a big cockroach,
The breast of his shirt he fixed it straight in—
'They'll think it's a diamond,' says Brian O'Linn!

Brian O'Linn went a-courting one night,
He set both the mother and daughter to fight—
'Stop, stop,' he exclaimed, 'if you have but the tin,
I'll marry you both,' says Brian O'Linn!

Brian O'Linn went to bring his wife home,
He had but one horse, that was all skin and bone—
'I'll put her behind me, as nate as a pin,
And her mother before me,' says Brian O'Linn!

Brian O'Linn and his wife and wife's mother,
They all crossed over the bridge together,
The bridge broke down and they all tumbled in—
'We'll go home by water,' says Brian O'Linn!

ANON

When good king Arthur ruled this land,
   He was a goodly king;
He stole three pecks of barley-meal,
   To make a bag-pudding.

A bag-pudding the king did make,
   And stuff'd it well with plums;
And in it put great lumps of fat,
   As big as my two thumbs.

The king and queen did eat thereof,
   And noblemen beside;
And what they could not eat that night,
   The queen next morning fried.

ANON

The Derby Ram

As I was going to Derby,
   'Twas on a market day,
I saw the finest ram, sir,
   That ever was fed on hay.
This ram was fat behind, sir,
   This ram was fat before,
This ram was ten yards high, sir,
   If he wasn't a little more.
      That's a lie, that's a lie,
      That's a tid i fa la lie.

Now the inside of this ram, sir,
   Would hold ten sacks of corn,
And you could turn a coach and six
   On the inside of his horn.
Now the wool upon his back, sir,
   It reached up to the sky,
And in it was a crow's next,
   For I heard the young ones cry.
      That's a lie, that's a lie,
      That's a tid i fa la lie.

45

Now the wool upon his belly, sir,
    Went draggling on the ground,
And that was took to Derby, sir,
    And sold for ten thousand pound.
Now the wool upon his tail, sir,
    Was ten inches and an ell,
And that was took to Derby, sir,
    To toll the old market-bell.
        That's a lie, that's a lie,
        That's a tid i fa la lie.

Now the man that fed this ram, sir,
    He fed him twice a day,
And each time that he fed him, sir,
    He ate a rick of hay.
Now the man that watered this ram, sir,
    He watered him twice a day,
And each time that he watered him
    He drank the river dry.
        That's a lie, that's a lie,
        That's a tid i fa la lie.

Now the butcher that killed the ram, sir,
    Was up to his knees in blood,
And the boy that held the bowl, sir,
    Got washed away in the flood.
Now all the boys in Derby, sir,
    Went begging for his eyes,
They kicked them up and down the street,
    For they were a good football size.
        That's a lie, that's a lie,
        That's a tid i fa la lie.

Now all the women of Derby, sir,
    Went begging for his ears,
To make their leather aprons of
    That lasted them forty years.

And the man that fatted the ram, sir,
  He must be very rich,
And the man that sung this song, sir,
  Is a lying son of a bitch.
    That's the truth, that's the truth,
    That's the tid i fa la truth.

ANON

The Red Herring

Herring and ling!
  O herring and ling!
Of all the fish in the sea
  Is Herring the king.

Oh, what do you think
  I made of his head?
I made as fine oven
  As ever baked bread.
Herring and ling, O herring and ling,
Don't you think I did well with my red herring?

Oh, what do you think
  I made of his fins?
I made a whole parcel
  Of needles and pins.
Herring and ling, O herring and ling,
Don't you think I did well with my red herring?

Oh, what do you think
  I made of his eyes?
I made a whole parcel
  Of puddings and pies.
Herring and ling, O herring and ling,
Don't you think I did well with my red herring?

Oh, what do you think
   I made of his back?
I made as fine whip
   As you ever did crack.
Herring and ling, O herring and ling,
Don't you think I did well with my red herring?

Oh, what do you think
   I made of his ribs?
I made fifty ox-stalls
   And fifty ox-cribs.
Herring and ling, O herring and ling,
Don't you think I did well with my red herring?

Oh, what do you think
   I made of his breast?
I made fifty good oxen
   As ever yoke pressed.
Herring and ling, O herring and ling.
Don't you think I did well with my red herring?

Oh, what do you think
   I made of his tail?
I made the best ship
   That ever set sail.
Herring and ling, O herring and ling.
Don't you think I did well with my red herring?

ANON

There was a man of Thessaly,
    And he was wondrous wise,
He jumped into a bramble bush
    And scratched out both his eyes.
And when he saw his eyes were out,
    With all his might and main
He jumped into another bush
    And scratched them in again.

ANON

[The Divine Blacksmith]

The Divine Blacksmith *in th'Abyss of Light*,
Yawning and lolling *with a careless beat*,
Struck out the mute Creation at a Heat.
But he work'd hard to Hammer out our Souls,
He blew the Bellows, and stir'd up the Coals;
Long time he thought, and could not on a sudden
Knead up with unskim' *Milk* this Reas'ning Pudding:
Tender and mild within its Bag it lay
Confessing still the softness of its Clay,
And kind as Milk-Maids on their Wedding-Day.
Till *Pride of Empire, Lust,* and hot Desire
Did over-boile him, like too great a Fire,
And understanding grown, *misunderstood*,
Burn'd Him to th'Pot, and sour'd his curdled Blood.

MATTHEW PRIOR

Il était un Petit Homme

Il était un p'tit homme
Qui s'appelait Guilleri,
    Carabi;

Il s'en fut à la chasse,
A la chasse aux perdrix,
          Carabi,
          Toto carabo.
Marchand d' carabas,
Compère Guilleri,
Te lairas-tu mouri?

Il s'en fut à la chasse,
A la chasse aux perdrix,
          Carabi;
Il monta sur un arbre
Pour voir ses chiens couri,
          Carabi;
          Toto carabo.
Marchand d' carabas,
Compère Guilleri,
Te lairas-tu mouri?

Il monta sur un arbre
Pour voir ses chiens couri,
          Carabi;
La branche vint à rompre,
Et Guilleri tombi,
          Carabi,
          Toto carabo.
Marchand d' carabas,
Compère Guilleri,
Te lairas-tu mouri?

La branche vint à rompre,
Et Guilleri tombi,
          Carabi;
Il se cassa la jambe,
Et le bras se démit,
          Carabi,

Toto carabo.
Marchand d' carabas,
Compère Guilleri,
Te lairas-tu mouri?

Il se cassa la jambe
Et le bras se démit,
Carabi;
Les dam's de l'Hôpital
Sont arrivé's au bruit,
Carabi,
Toto carabo.
Marchand d' carabas,
Compère Guilleri,
Te lairas-tu mouri?

Les dam's de l'Hôpital
Sont arrivé's au bruit,
Carabi;
L'une apporte un emplâtre,
L'autre, de la charpi,
Carabi,
Toto carabo.
Marchand d' carabas,
Compère Guilleri,
Te lairas-tu mouri?

L'une apporte un emplâtre,
L'autre, de la charpi,
Carabi;
On lui banda la jambe
Et le bras lui remit,
Carabi,
Toto carabo.
Marchand d' carabas,
Compère Guilleri
Te lairas-tu mouri?

On lui banda la jambe,
Et le bras lui remit,
        Carabi;
Pour remercier ces dames,
Guilleri les embrassi,
        Carabi,
            Toto carabo.
Marchand d'carabas,
Compère Guilleri,
Te lairas-tu mouri?

Pour remercier ces dames,
Guilleri les embrassi,
        Carabi,
Ca prouv' que par les femmes
L'homme est toujours guéri;
        Carabi,
            Toto carabo.
Marchand d' carabas.
Compère Guilleri,
Te lairas-tu mouri?

ANON

Namby-Pamby

*A Panegyric on the New Verisification
Address'd to A --- P ---, Esq.*

*Naughty Paughty Jack-a-Dandy,
Stole a Piece of Sugar Candy
From the Grocer's Shoppy-Shop,
And away did hoppy-hop.*

All ye poets of the age,
All ye witlings of the stage,

Learn your jingles to reform,
Crop your numbers to conform.
Let your little verses flow
Gently, sweetly, row by row;
Let the verse the subject fit,
Little subject, little wit.
Namby-Pamby is your guide,
Albion's joy, Hibernia's pride.
Namby-Pamby, pilly-piss,
Rhimy-pim'd on Missy Miss
Tartaretta Tartaree,
From the navel to the knee;
That her father's gracy-grace
Might give him a placey place.

   He no longer writes of Mammy
Andromache and her lammy,
Hanging-panging at the breast
Of a matron most distress'd.
Now the venal poet sings
Baby clouts and baby things,
Baby dolls and baby houses,
Little misses, little spouses,
Little playthings, little toys,
Little girls and little boys.
As an actor does his part,
So the nurses get by heart
Namby-Pamby's little rhimes,
Little jingles, little chimes,
To repeat to missy-miss,
Piddling ponds of pissy-piss;
Cracking-packing like a lady,
Or bye-bying in the crady.
Namby-Pamby's doubly mild,
Once a man, and twice a child;
To his hanging sleeves restor'd,
Now he foots it like a lord;

Now he pumps his little wits,
Shitting writes, and writing shits,
All by little tiny bits.
And methinks I hear him say,
Boys and girls, come out to play!
Moon do's shine as bright as day.

Now my Namby-Pamby's found
Sitting on the friar's ground,
Picking silver, picking gold;
Namby-Pamby's never old.
Bally-cally, they begin,
Namby-Pamby still keeps in.
Namby-Pamby is no clown.
London Bridge is broken down:
Now he courts the gay ladee,
Dancing o'er the Lady-Lee.
Now he sings of Lick-spit Lyar,
Burning in the brimstone fire;
Lyar, lyar! Lick-spit, Lick,
Turn about the candle stick!
Now he sings of Jacky Horner,
Sitting in the chimney corner,
Eating of a Christmas pye,
Putting in his thumb, O fie!
Putting in, O fie! his thumb,
Pulling out, O strange, a plum.
Now he plays at Stee-Staw-Stud,
Sticking apples in the mud;
When 'tis turn'd to Stee-Staw-Stire,
Then he sticks them in the mire,
Now he acts the grenadier,
Calling for a pot of beer.
Where's his money? He's forgot;
Get him gone, a drunken sot.
Now a cock-horse does he ride,
And anon on timber stride.

See and Saw, and Sacch'ry Down,
London is a gallant town!
Now he gathers riches in,
Thicker, faster, pin by pin;
Pins apiece to see his show,
Boys and girls flock row by row;
From their clothes the pins they take,
Risk a whipping for his sake;
From their cloaths the pins they pull
To fill Namby's cushion full.
So much wit at such an age
Does a genius great presage;
Second childhood gone and past,
Should he prove a man at last,
What must second manhood be
In a child so bright as he.

Guard him, ye poetic pow'rs,
Watch his minutes, watch his hours;
Let your tuneful nine inspire him;
Let the poets, one and all,
To his genius victims fall.

HENRY CAREY

Monsieur de la Palisse

Messieurs, vous plait-il d'ouir
L'air du fameux La Palisse?
Il pourra vous réjouir,
Pourvu qu'il vous divertisse.
La Palisse eut bien peu de biens,
Pour soutenir sa naissance;
Mais il ne manqua de rien,
Tant qu'il fut dans l'abondance.

Bien instruit dès le berceau,
Jamais, tant il fut honnête,
Il ne mettait son chapeau,
Qu'il ne se couvrit la tête.
Il était affable et doux.
De l'humeur de feu son père
Et n'entrait guère en courroux,
Si ce n'est dans la colère.

Ses valets étaient soigneux
De le servir d'andouillettes,
Et n'oubliaient pas les oeufs
Surtout dans les omelettes.
De l'inventeur du raisin
Il révérait la mémoire;
Et pour bien goûter le vin,
Jugait qu'il fallait en boire.

Il disait que le nouveau
Avait pour lui plus d'amorce;
Et moins il y mettait d'eau
Plus il y trouvait de force.
Il consultait rarement
Hippocrate et sa doctrine,
Et se purgeait seulement
Lorsqu'il prenait médecine.

Il aimait à prendre l'air
Quand la saison était bonne,
Et n'attendait pas l'hiver
Pour vendanger en automne.
Il épousa, ce dit-on,
Une vertueuse dame;
S'il était resté garçon,
Il n'aurait pas eu de femme.

Il en fut toujours chéri;
Elle n'était pas jalouse;
Sitôt qu'il fut son mari,
Elle devint son épouse.
D'un air galant et badin,
Il courtisait sa Caliste,
Sans jamais être chagrin
Qu'au moment qu'il était triste.

Il brillait comme un soleil,
Sa chevelure était blonde;
Il n'eût pas eu son pareil,
S'il eût été seul au monde.
Il eut des talents divers;
Même on assure une chose:
Quand il écrivait des vers
Il n'écrivait pas en prose.

Il voyageait volontiers,
Courant par tout le royaume;
Quand il était à Poitiers,
Il n'était pas à Vendôme.
Il se plaisait en bateau,
Et soit en paix, soit en guerre,
Il allait toujours par eau,
Quand il n'allait pas par terre.

Il choisissait prudemment
De deux choses la meilleure;
Et répétait fréquemment
Ce qu'il disait à toute heure.
Il fut, à la vérité,
Un danseur assez vulgaire;
Mais il n'eût pas mal chanté,
S'il n'avait voulu se taire.

Regretté de ses soldats,
Il mourut digne d'envie;
Et le jour de son trépas
Fut le dernier de sa vie.
Il mourut le vendredi,
Le dernier jour de son âge;
S'il fût mort le samedi,
Il eût vécu davantage.

ANON

An Elegy on that Glory of her Sex, Mrs. Mary Blaize

Good people all, with one accord,
  Lament for Madame BLAIZE,
Who never wanted a good word—
  From those who spoke her praise.

The needy seldom passed her door,
  And always found her kind;
She freely lent to all the poor,—
  Who left a pledge behind.

She strove the neighbourhood to please,
  With manners wondrous winning,
And never followed wicked ways,—
  Unless when she was sinning.

At church, in silks and satins new,
  With hoop of monstrous size,
She never slumbered in her pew,—
  But when she shut her eyes.

Her love was sought, I do aver,
    By twenty beaux and more;
The king himself has followed her,—
    When she has walked before.

But now her wealth and finery fled,
    Her hangers-on cut short all;
The doctors found, when she was dead,—
    Her last disorder mortal.

Let us lament, in sorrow sore,
    For Kent-Street well may say,
That had she lived a twelve-month more,—
    She had not died to-day.

OLIVER GOLDSMITH

The Grand Panjandrum

So she went into the garden to cut a cabbage leaf, to make an apple pie; and at the same time a great she-bear coming up the street, pops its head into the shop, 'What! no soap?' So he died, and she very imprudently married the barber; and there were present the Picninnies, and the Joblillies, and the Garyulies, and the grand Panjandrum himself, with the little round button at top; and they all fell to playing the game of catch as catch can, till the gunpowder ran out at the heels of their boots.

SAMUEL FOOTE: 1755

from *An Island in the Moon*

1. *[Suction's Anthem]*

I say this evening we'll all get drunk. I say dash,
An Anthem an Anthem, said Suction.
        Lo the Bat with Leathern wing
        Winking & blinking
        Winking & blinking
        Winking & blinking
        Like Doctor Johnson.

Quid—O ho said Doctor Johnson
        To Scipio Africanus
        If you don't own me a Philosopher
        I'll kick your Roman Anus.

Suction—A ha to Doctor Johnson
        Said Scipio Africanus
        Lift up my Roman Petticoat
        And kiss my Roman Anus.

And the Cellar goes down with a Step (Grand Chorus).

2. *[Quid the Cynic's Song]*

[1]

When old corruption first begun,
    Adorn'd in yellow vest,
He committed on flesh a whoredom—
    O, what a wicked beast!

[2]

From them a callow babe did spring,
    And old corruption smil'd
To think his race should never end,
    For now he had a child.

[3]

He call'd him surgery, & fed
    The babe with his own milk,
For flesh & he could n'er agree,
    She would not let him suck.

[4]

And this he always kept in mind,
    And form'd a crooked knife,
And ran about with bloody hands
    To seek his mother's life.

[5]

And as he ran to seek his mother
    He met with a dead woman,
He fell in love & married her,
    A deed which is not common.

[6]

She soon grew pregnant & brought forth
    Scurvy & spott'd fever.
The father grin'd & skipt about,
    And said, 'I'm made for ever!'

[7]

'For now I have procur'd these imps
    I'll try experiments.'
With that he tied poor scurvy down
    & stopt up all its vents.

[8]

And when the child began to swell,
    He shouted out aloud,
'I've found the dropsy out, & soon,
    Shall do the world more good.'

He took up fever by the neck
    And cut out all its spots,
And thro' the holes which he had made
    He first discover'd guts.

3. [In Obtuse Angle's Study]

Obtuse Angle, Scopprell, Aradobo, & Tilly Lally are all met in Obtuse Angle's study.

'Pray,' said Aradobo, 'is Chatterton a Mathematician?'

'No,' said Obtuse Angle. 'How can you be so foolish as to think he was?'

'Oh, I did not think he was—I only ask'd,' said Aradobo.

'How could you think he was not, & ask if he was?' said Obtuse Angle.

'Oh no, Sir. I did think he was, before you told me, but afterwards I thought he was not.'

Obtuse Angle said, 'In the first place you thought he was, & then afterwards when I said he was not, you thought he was not. Why, I know that——'

'Oh no, sir, I thought that he was not, but I ask'd to know whether he was.'

'How can that be?' said Obtuse Angle. 'How could you ask & think that he was not?'

'Why,' said he, 'it came into my head that he was not.'

'Why then,' said Obtuse Angle, 'you said that he was.'

'Did I say so? Law! I did not think I said that.'

'Did not he?' said Obtuse Angle.

'Yes,' said Scopprell.

'But I meant——' said Aradobo, 'I—I—I can't think. Law! Sir, I wish you'd tell me how it is.'

Then Obtuse Angle put his chin in his hand &

said, 'Whenever you think, you must always think for yourself.'

'How, sir?' said Aradobo. 'Whenever I think, I must think myself? I think I do. In the first place——' said he with a grin.

'Poo! Poo!' said Obtuse Angle. 'Don't be a fool.'

Then Tilly Lally took up a Quadrant & ask'd, 'Is not this a sun-dial?'

'Yes,' said Scopprell, 'but it's broke.'

At this moment the three Philosophers enter'd, and low'ring darkness hover'd over the assembly.

'Come,' said the Epicurean, 'let's have some rum & water, & hang the mathematics! Come, Aradobo! Say some thing.'

Then Aradobo began, 'In the first place I think, I think in the first place that Chatterton was clever at Fissie Follogy, Pistinology, Aridology, Arography, Transmography, Phizography, Hogamy, Hatomy, & hall that, but, in the first place, he eat every little, wickly—that is, he slept very little, which he brought into a consumsion; & what was that that he took? Fissie or somethink,—& so died!'

So all the people in the book enter'd into the room, & they could not talk any more to the present purpose.

4. [Sipsop's Song]

Hang your serious songs, said Sipsop & he sung as follows
        Fa ra so bo ro
         Fa ra bo ra
        Sa ba ra ra ba rare roro
        Sa ra ra ra bo ro ro ro
        Radara
        Sarapodo no flo ro

WILLIAM BLAKE

Not Ragged-and-Tough

Ragged-and-Tough.

Not Ragged-and-Tough,
But—
  Huckem-a-Buff,
First cousin to Ragged-and-Tough.

Not Ragged-and-Tough
Nor Huckem-a-Buff
First cousin to Ragged-and-Tough,
But—
  Miss Grizzle,
Maiden aunt to Huckem-a-Buff
First cousin to Ragged-and-Tough.

Not Ragged-and-Tough
Nor Huckem-a-Buff
First cousin to Ragged-and-Tough
Nor Miss Grizzle, maiden aunt to Huckem-a-Buff
First cousin to Ragged-and-Tough,
But—
  Goody Gherkin,
Grandmama to Miss Grizzle
Maiden aunt to Huckem-a-Buff
First cousin to Ragged-and-Tough.

Not Ragged-and-Tough
Nor Huckem-a-Buff
First cousin to Ragged-and-Tough,
Nor Miss Grizzle, maiden aunt to Huckem-a-Buff
First cousin to Ragged-and-Tough,
Nor Goody Gherkin, grandmama to Miss Grizzle
Maiden aunt to Huckem-a-Buff
First cousin to Ragged-and-Tough,

But—
    Little Snap,
Favourite dog of Goody Gherkin
Grandmama to Miss Grizzle
Maiden aunt to Huckem-a-Buff
First cousin to Ragged-and-Tough.
Not Ragged-and-Tough
Nor Huckem-a-Buff
First cousin to Ragged-and-Tough,
Nor Miss Grizzle, maiden aunt to Huckem-a-Buff
First cousin to Ragged-and-Tough,
Nor Goody Gherkin, grandmama to Miss Grizzle
Maiden aunt to Huckem-a-Buff
First cousin to Ragged-and-Tough,
Nor Little Snap, favourite dog of Goody Gherkin
Grandmama to Miss Grizzle
Maiden aunt to Huckem-a-Buff
First cousin to Ragged-and-Tough,
But—
    the Whip,
Which tickled the tail of Little Snap,
Favourite dog of Goody Gherkin,
Grandmama to Miss Grizzle,
Maiden aunt to Huckem-a-Buff,
First cousin to Ragged-and-Tough.

ANON

We're All in the Dumps

We're all in the dumps,
For diamonds are trumps,
The kittens are gone to St. Paul's,
The babies are bit,
The moon's in a fit
And the houses are built without walls.

ANON

Fower-an-twenty Hielandmen

Fower-an-twenty Hielandmen
Were ridin on a snail,
When up cam the hinmaist
An trampit on her tail.
O, the snail shot oot her wee bit horns,
Jist like a hummel coo,
'Hech!' quo' the foremaist, 'we'll a be stickit noo!'

Fower-an-twenty tailor lads
Were fechtin wi a slug,
'Hallo, sirs!' said ane o them,
'Jist haud him by the lug!'
But the beastie frae his shell cam oot,
An shook his fearsome heid,
'Rin, rin, my tailors bold,
Or we will a be deid!'

I gaed by the mill door,
When oot cam Miller Reid,
His cap upon his feet,
An his breeks upon his heid.
Noo, I've sung ye a' a sang,
An I've telt ye a' a tale,
An it's a big lees
Frae the heid tae the tail.

ANON

Les Trois Limaçons

J'ai rencontré trois limaces
Qui labouraient mon pré,
Venez tous voir,
Qui labouraient mon pré.
Ne venez pas.

66

Je suis allé un peu plu loin,
J'ai rencontré une ânesse
 Qui racommodait son bât,
      Venez tous voir,
 Qui raccommodait son bât,
      Ne venez pas.

Je suis allé un peu plus loin,
J'ai rencontré une église
Qui n'avait ni prêtre, ni curé,
      Venez tous voir,
Qui n'avait ni prêtre ni curé,
      Ne venez pas.

Il n'y avait qu'une vieille chèvre
Qui chantait 'Alleluia',
      Venez tous voir,
Qui chantait 'Alleluia'.
      Ne venez pas.

Il y avait un loup derrière la porte
Qui voulait la confesser,
      Venez tous voir,
Qui voulait la confesser.
      Ne venez pas.

                                        ANON

I sit with my toes in the brook,
And if anyone asks me why
I give him a tap with my crook,
Necessity drives me, say I.

                                        ANON

I put my hat upon my head
  And walk'd into the Strand,
And there I met another man
  Whose hat was in his hand.

SAMUEL JOHNSON

Aiken Drum

There was a man lived in the moon, lived in the moon, lived
    in the moon,
There was a man lived in the moon,
And his name was Aiken Drum;
    And he played upon a ladle, a ladle, a ladle,
    And he played upon a ladle,
    And his name was Aiken Drum.

And his hat was made of good cream cheese, good cream
    cheese, good cream cheese,
And his hat was made of good cream cheese,
And his name was Aiken Drum.

And his coat was made of good roast beef, good roast beef,
    good roast beef,
And his coat was made of good roast beef,
And his name was Aiken Drum.

And his buttons were made of penny loaves, penny loaves,
    penny loaves,
And his buttons were made of penny loaves,
And his name was Aiken Drum.

His waistcoat was made of crust of pies, crust of pies, crust
    of pies,
His waistcoat was made of crust of pies,
And his name was Aiken Drum.

His breeches were made of haggis bags, haggis bags, haggis
    bags,
His breeches were made of haggis bags,
And his name was Aiken Drum.

There was a man in another town, another town, another
    town,
There was a man in another town,
And his name was Willy Wood;
    And he played upon a razor, a razor, a razor,
    And he played upon a razor,
    And his name was Willy Wood.

And he ate up all the good cream cheese, good cream cheese,
    good cream cheese,
And he ate up all the good cream cheese,
And his name was Willy Wood.

And he ate up all the good roast beef, good roast beef, good
    roast beef,
And he ate up all the good roast beef,
And his name was Willy Wood.

And he ate up all the penny loaves, penny loaves, penny
    loaves,
And he ate up all the penny loaves,
And his name was Willy Wood.

And he ate up all the good pie crust, good pie crust, good pie
    crust,
And he ate up all the good pie crust,
And his name was Willy Wood.

But he choked upon the haggis bags, haggis bags, haggis bags,
But he choked upon the haggis bags,
And that ended Willy Wood.

ANON

Sonnet Found in a Deserted Mad-house

Oh that my soul a marrow-bone might seize!
For the old egg of my desire is broken,
Spilled is the pearly white and spilled the yolk, and
As the mild melancholy contents grease
My path the shorn lamb baas like bumblebees.
Time's trashy purse is as a taken token
Or like a thrilling recitation, spoken
By mournful mouths filled full of mirth and cheese.

And yet, why should I clasp the earthful urn?
Or find the frittered fig that felt the fast?
Or choose to chase the cheese around the churn?
Or swallow any pill from out the past?
Ah, no Love, not while your hot kisses burn
Like a potato riding on the blast.

ANON

Hoddley, poddley, puddle and fogs,
Cats are to marry the poodle dogs;
Cats in blue jackets and dogs in red hats,
What will become of the mice and rats?

ANON

Three Young Rats

Three young rats with black felt hats,
Three young ducks with white straw flats,
Three young dogs with curling tails,
Three young cats with demi-veils,
Went out to walk with two young pigs
In satin vests and sorrel wigs;
But suddenly it chanced to rain,
And so they all went home again.

ANON

As I went up the humber jumber,
    Humber jumber jeenio,
There I met Sir Hoker Poker
    Carrying away campeenio.

If I had had my tit-my-tat,
    My tit-my-tat my teenio,
I'd never have let Sir Hoker Poker
    Carry away campeenio.

                                ANON

I saw Esau sawing wood,
And Esau saw I saw him;
Though Esau saw I saw him saw,
Still Esau went on sawing.

                                ANON

from *The Loves of the Triangles*

Stay your rude steps, or e'er your feet invade
The Muses' haunts, ye sons of War and Trade!
Nor you, ye Legion Fiends of Church and Law,
Pollute these pages with unhallow'd paw!
Debased, corrupted, grovelling, and confined,
No DEFINITIONS touch *your* senseless mind;
To *you* no POSTULATES prefer their claim,
No ardent AXIOMS your dull souls inflame;
For *you* no TANGENTS touch, no ANGLES meet,
No CIRCLES join in osculation sweet!
   For *me*, ye CISSOIDS, round my temples bend
Your wandering Curves; ye CONCHOIDS extend;
Let playful PENDULES quick vibration feel,
While silent CYCLOID rests upon her wheel;
Let HYDROSTATICS, simpering as they go,

71

Lead these light Naiads on fantastic toe;
Let shrill ACOUSTICS tune the tiny lyre;
With EUCLID sage fair ALGEBRA conspire;
The obedient pulley strong MECHANICS ply,
And wanton OPTICS roll the melting eye!

JOHN HOOKHAM FRERE: 1798

Ipecacuanha

Coughing in a shady grove
   Sat my Juliana,
Lozenges I gave my love,
   Ipecacuanha—
Full twenty from the lozenge box
   The greedy nymph did pick;
Then, sighing sadly, said to me—
   My Damon, I am sick

GEORGE CANNING

from *The Progress of Man*

Mark the dark rook, on pendent branches hung,
With anxious fondness feed her cawing young.—
Mark the fell leopard through the desert prowl,
Fish prey on fish, and fowl regale on fowl;
How Lybian tigers' chawdrons love assails,
And warms, midst seas of ice, the melting whales;—
Cools the crimpt cod, fierce pangs to perch imparts,
Shrinks shrivell'd shrimps, but opens oysters' hearts;—
Then say, how all these things together tend
To one great truth, prime object, and good end?
  First—to each living thing, whate'er its kind,
Some lot, some part, some station is assign'd.
The feather'd race with pinions skim the *air*—

Not so the mackarel, and still less the bear:
This roams the *wood*, carniv'rous for his prey;
That with soft roe, pursues his *watery* way:—
This slain by hunters yields his shaggy hide;
That caught by fishers, is on *Sundays* cried.—

But each contented with his humble sphere,
Moves unambitious through the circling year;
Nor e'er forgets the fortune of his race,
Nor pines to quit, or strives to change his place.
Ah! who has seen the mailed lobster rise,
Clap her broad wings, and soaring claim the skies?
When did the owl, descending from her bow'r,
Crop, 'midst the fleecy flocks, the tender flower;
Or the young heifer plunge, with pliant limb,
In the salt wave, and fish-like strive to swim?

The same with plants—potatoes 'tatoes breed—
Uncostly cabbage springs from cabbage seed,
Lettuces, to lettuce, leeks to leeks succeed;
Nor e'er did cooling cucumbers presume
To flow'r like myrtle, or like violets bloom,
—Man, only—rash, refined, presumptuous Man,
Starts from his rank, and mars creation's plan.

GEORGE CANNING: 1798

Song by Rogero, in The Rovers

Whene'er with haggard eyes I view
    This Dungeon, that I'm rotting in,
I think of those Companions true
    Who studied with me at the U—
        —NIVERSITY of *Gottingen*,—
        —NIVERSITY of *Gottingen*.

Sweet kerchief, check'd with heav'nly blue,
  Which once my love sat knotting in!—
Alas! MATILDA *then* was true!—
  At least I thought so at the U—
      —NIVERSITY of *Gottingen*—
      —NIVERSITY of *Gottingen*.

Barbs! Barbs! alas! how swift you flew
  Her neat Post-Waggon trotting in!
Ye bore MATILDA from my view.
  Forlorn I languish'd at the U—
      —NIVERSITY of *Gottingen*—
      —NIVERSITY of *Gottingen*.

This faded form! this pallid hue!
  This blood my veins is clotting in.
My years are many—They were few
  When first I entered at the U—
      —NIVERSITY of *Gottingen*—
      —NIVERSITY of *Gottingen*.

There first for thee my passion grew,
  Sweet! sweet MATILDA POTTINGEN!
Thou wast the daughter of my TU-
  —TOR, *Law Professor* at the U—
      —NIVERSITY of *Gottingen*!—
      —NIVERSITY of *Gottingen*!—

Sun, moon, and thou vain world, adieu,
  That kings and priests are plotting in:
Here doom'd to starve on water-gru—
  —el, never shall I see the U—
      —NIVERSITY of *Gottingen*—
      —NIVERSITY of *Gottingen*.

GEORGE CANNING

74

Lunar Stanzas

Night saw the crew like pedlars with their packs,
   Altho' it were too dear to pay for eggs,
Walk crank along with coffin on their backs
   While in their arms they bow their weary legs.

And yet 'twas strange, and scarce can one suppose
   That a brown buzzard-fly should steal and wear
His white jean breeches and black woollen hose,
   But thence that flies have souls is very clear.

But, Holy Father! what shall save the soul,
   When cobblers ask three dollars for their shoes?
When cooks their biscuits with a shot-tower roll,
   And farmers rake their hay-cocks with their hoes.

Yet, 'twere profuse to see for pendant light
   A tea-pot dangle in a lady's ear;
And 'twere indelicate, although she might
   Swallow two whales and yet the moon shine clear.

But what to me are woven clouds, or what,
   If dames from spiders learn to warp their looms?
If coal-black ghosts turn soldiers for the State,
   With wooden eyes and lightning-rods for plumes?

Oh! too, too shocking! barbarous savage taste!
   To eat one's mother ere itself was born!
To gripe the tall town steeple by the waist,
   And scoop it out to be his drinking-horn.

No more; no more! I'm sick and dead and gone;
   Boxed in a coffin, stifled six feet deep;
Thorns, fat and fearless, prick my skin and bone,
   And revel o'er me, like a soulless sheep.

HENRY COGGSWELL KNIGHT: 1815

[One Old Ox]

One old Oxford ox opening oysters;
Two tee-totums totally tired of trying to trot to Tadbury;
Three tall tigers tippling tenpenny tea;
Four fat friars fanning fainting flies;
Five frippy Frenchmen foolishly fishing for flies;
Six sportsmen shooting snipes;
Seven Severn salmons swallowing shrimps;
Eight Englishmen eagerly examining Europe;
Nine nimble noblemen nibbling nonpareils;
Ten tinkers tinkling upon ten tin tinder-boxes with ten
    tenpenny tacks;
Eleven elephants elegantly equipt;
Twelve typographical topographers typically translating types.

ANON

The Dead Pig

T' owd pig's got mezzles an' she's deead, poor thing.
An' what will you mak o' her poor awd heead?
'T will mak as good a yune as iver baked breead.
An' what will you mak o' her poor awd legs?
As good a set o' bed-props as iver propped beds.
An' what will you mak o' her poor awd skin?
'Twill mak as good a blanket as iver man lay in.
An' what will you mak o' her poor awd tail?
'Twill mak as good a hammer-shaft as iver drove a nail.
An' what will you mak of her poor awd lugs?
As good a pair o' bed-flops as iver flopped bugs.

ANON

[Eaper Weaper]

Eaper weaper, chimbley-sweeper,
Had a wife but couldn't keep her,
Had anovver, didn't love her,
Up the chimbley he did shove her.

ANON

[The Owl in the Oak]

In an oak there liv'd an owl,
 Frisky, whisky, wheedle!
She thought herself a clever fowl;
 Fiddle, faddle, feedle.

Her face alone her wisdom shew,
 Frisky, whisky, wheedle!
For all she said was, Whit te whoo!
 Fiddle, faddle, feedle.

Her silly note a gunner heard,
 Frisky, whisky, wheedle!
Says he, I'll shoot you, stupid bird!
 Fiddle, faddle, feedle.

Now if he had not heard her hoot,
 Frisky, whisky, wheedle,
He had not found her out to shoot,
 Fiddle, faddle, feedle.

ANON: 1807

77

The Muses

Musa, Musae,
The Gods were at tea:
Musae, Musam,
Eating raspberry jam:
Musa, Musā,
Made by Cupid's mamma.

ANON

Nottamun Town

In Nottamun Town not a soul would look up,
Not a soul would look up, not a soul would look down,
Not a soul would look up, not a soul would look down
To tell me the way to Nottamun Town.

I rode a big horse that was called a grey mare,
Grey mane and tail, grey stripes down his back,
Grey mane and tail, grey stripes down his back,
There weren't a hair on him but what was called black.

She stood so still, she threw me to the dirt,
She tore my hide and bruised my shirt;
From stirrup to stirrup, I mounted again
And on my ten toes I rode over the plain

Met the King and the Queen and a company of men
A-walking behind and a-riding before.
A stark naked drummer came walking along
With his hands in his bosom a-beating his drum.

Sat down on a hot and cold frozen stone,
Ten thousand stood round me and I was alone.
Took my heart in my hand to keep my head warm.
Ten thousand got drowned that never were born.

ANON

There was an old soldier of Bicester
Was walking one day with his sister.
  A bull, with one poke,
   Toss'd her into an oak,
Before the old gentleman miss'd her.

ANON: 1822

Shadrach
Shake the bed;
Meshech
Make the bed;
And Abednego,
And to bed we go.

ANON

Mistress Towl

There was an Old Woman named Towl
Who went out to sea with her Owl,
  But the Owl was sea-sick
   And screamed for physic;
Which sadly annoyed Mistress Towl.

ANON: 1820

Old Woman of Harrow

There was an Old Woman of Harrow,
Who visited in a wheelbarrow,
  And her servant before
   Knock'd loud at each door
To announce the Old Woman of Harrow.

ANON: 1820

Oh, dear, what can the matter be?
Two old women got up in an apple-tree;
One came down,
And the other stayed till Saturday.

ANON

Dame Wiggins of Lee
and her Seven Wonderful Cats

Dame Wiggins of Lee
Was a worthy old soul,
As e'er threaded a nee-
dle, or wash'd in a bowl:
She held mice and rats
In such antipa-thy
That seven fine cats
Kept Dame Wiggins of Lee.

The rats and mice scared
By this fierce whisker'd crew,
The seven poor cats
Soon had nothing to do;
So, as any one idle
She ne'er loved to see,
She sent them to school,
Did Dame Wiggins of Lee.

But soon she grew tired
Of living alone;
So she sent for her cats
From school to come home.
Each rowing a wherry,
Returning you see:
The frolic made merry
Dame Wiggins of Lee.

The Dame was quite pleas'd,
And ran out to market;
When she came back
They were mending the carpet.
The needle each handled
As brisk as a bee;
'Well done, my good cats,'
Said Dame Wiggins of Lee.

To give them a treat,
She ran out for some rice;
When she came back,
They were skating on ice.
'I shall soon see one drown,
Aye, perhaps, two or three,
I'll bet half-a-crown,'
Said Dame Wiggins of Lee.

They called the next day
On the tomtit and sparrow,
And wheeled a poor sick lamb
Home in a barrow.
'You shall all have some sprats
For your human-ity,
My seven good cats,'
Said Dame Wiggins of Lee.

While she ran to the fields,
To look for its dam,
They were warming the bed
For the poor sick lamb:
They'd turned up the clothes
All as neat as could be;
'I shall ne'er want a nurse,'
Said Dame Wiggins of Lee.

She wished them good night,
And went up to bed;
When, lo! in the morning,
The cats were all fled.
But soon—what a fuss!
'Where can they all be?
Here, pussy, puss, puss!'
Cried Dame Wiggins of Lee.

The Dame's heart was nigh broke,
So she sat down to weep,
When she saw them come back
Each riding a sheep;
She fondled and patted
Each purring Tom-my:
'Ah! welcome, my dears,'
Said Dame Wiggins of Lee.

The Dame was unable
Her pleasure to smother;
To see the sick Lamb
Jump up to its mother
In spite of the gout,
And a pain in her knee,
She went dancing about:
Did Dame Wiggins of Lee.

The Farmer soon heard
Where his sheep went astray,
And arrived at Dame's door
With his faithful dog Tray.
He knocked with his crook,
And the stranger to see,
Out of window did look
Dame Wiggins of Lee.

For their kindness he had them
All drawn by his team;
And gave them some field-mice,
And raspberry-cream.
Said he, 'All my stock
You shall presently see;
For I honour the cats
Of Dame Wiggins of Lee.'

He sent his maid out
For some muffins and crumpets;
And when he turn'd round
They were playing of trumpets.
Said he, 'I suppose,
She's as deaf as can be,
Or this ne'er could be born
By Dame Wiggins of Lee.'

To show them his poultry,
He turn'd them all loose,
When each nimbly leap'd
On the back of a Goose,
Which frighten'd them so
That they ran to the sea,
And half-drown'd the poor cats
Of Dame Wiggins of Lee.

For their care of his lamb,
And their comical pranks,
He gave them a ham
And abundance of thanks.
'I wish you good-day,
My fine fellows,' said he:
'My compliments, pray,
To Dame Wiggins of Lee.'

You see them arrived
At their Dame's welcome door;
They show her their presents,
And all their good store.
'Now come in to supper,
And sit down with me;
All welcome once more,'
Cried Dame Wiggins of Lee.

MRS. PEARSON and
RICHARD SCRAFTON SHARPE

A child that has a cold we may suppose
Like wintry weather—Why?—It blows its nose.

THOMAS DIBDIN

Three wise men of Gotham,
They went to sea in a bowl,
And if the bowl had been stronger
My song had been longer.

ANON

The Wise Men of Gotham

By S. T. C., Professor of Mysticism
ΣΚΙΑΣ ΟΝΑΡ. – *Pindar*

In a bowl to sea went wise men three
On a brilliant night of June:
They carried a net, and their hearts were set
On fishing up the moon.

The sea was calm, the air was balm,
    Not a breath stirred low or high,
And the moon, I trow, lay as bright below,
    And as round as in the sky.

The wise men with the current went,
    Nor paddle nor oar had they,
And still as the grave they went on the wave,
    That they might not disturb their prey.

Far, far at sea, were the wise men three,
    When their fishing net they threw;
And at their throw, the moon below
    In a thousand fragments flew.

The sea was bright with the dancing light
    Of a milliom million gleams,
Which the broken moon shot forth as soon
    As the net disturbed her beams.

They drew in their net it was empty and wet:
    And they had lost their pain,
Soon ceased the play of each dancing ray,
    And the image was round again.

Three times they threw, three times they drew,
    And all the while were mute;
And ever anew their wonder grew,
    Till they could not but dispute.

Their silence they broke, and each one spoke
    Full long, and loud, and clear;
A man at sea their voices three
    Full three leagues off might hear.

The three wise men got home again
  To their children and their wives:
But touching their trip, and their net's vain dip,
  They disputed all their lives.

The wise men three could never agree,
  Why they missed the promised boon;
They agreed alone that their net they had thrown,
  And they had not caught the moon. . . .

THOMAS LOVE PEACOCK

The Carelesse Nurse Mayd

I sawe a Mayd sitte on a Bank,
Beguiled by Wooer fayne and fond;
And whiles His flatterynge Vowes She drank,
Her Nurselynge slipt within a Pond!

All Even Tide they Talkde and Kist,
For She was fayre and He was Kinde;
The Sunne went down before She wist
Another Sonne had sett behinde!

With angrie Hands and frownynge Browe,
That deemd Her owne the Urchine's Sinne,
She pluckt Him out, but he was nowe
Past being Whipt for fallynge in.

She then beginnes to wayle the Ladde
With Shrikes that Echo answerde round—
O! foolishe Mayd to be soe sadde
The Momente that her Care was drownd!

THOMAS HOOD

Ode to the Cameleopard

Welcome to Freedom's birth-place—and a den!
　　Great Anti-climax, hail!
So very lofty in thy front—but then,
　　So dwindling at the tail!—
In truth, thou hast the most unequal legs:
Has one pair gallop'd, whilst the other trotted,
Along with other brethren, leopard-spotted,
O'er Afric sand, where ostriches lay eggs?
Sure thou wert caught in some hard uphill chase,
Those hinder heels still keeping thee in check!
　　And yet thou seem'st prepar'd in any case,
　　Tho' they had lost the race,
　　　To win it—by a neck!

That lengthy neck—how like a crane's it looks!
Art thou the overseer of all the brutes?
Or dost thou browze on tip-top leaves or fruits—
Or go a-bird-nesting amongst the rooks?
How kindly nature caters for all wants;
Thus giving unto thee a neck that stretches,
　　And high food fetches—
To some a long nose, like the elephant's!

Oh! had'st thou any organ to thy bellows,
To turn they breath to speech in human style,
　　What secrets thou might'st tell us,
Where now our scientific guesses fail;
　　For instance, of the Nile,
Whether those Seven Mouths have any tail—
　　Mayhap thy luck too,
From that high head, as from a lofty hill,
Has let thee see the marvellous Timbuctoo—
Or drink of Niger at its infant rill;

What were the travels of our Major Denham,
    Or Clapperton, to thine
    In that same line,
If thou could'st only squat thee down and pen 'em!

Strange sights, indeed, thou must have overlook'd,
With eyes held ever in such vantage-stations!
Hast seen, perchance, unhappy white folks cook'd,
And then made free of negro corporations?
Poor wretches saved from cast away three deckers—
    By sooty wreckers—
From hungry waves to have a loss still drearier,
To far exceed the utmost aim of Park—
And find themselves, alas! beyond the mark,
In the *insides* of Africa's Interior!

Live on, Giraffe! genteelest of raff kind!—
Admir'd by noble and by royal tongues!—
    May no pernicious wind,
Or English fog, blight thy exotic lungs!
Live on in happy peace, altho' a rarity,
Nor envy thy poor cousin's more outrageous
    Parisian popularity;—
Whose very leopard-rash is grown contagious,
And worn on gloves and ribbons all about,
    Alas! they'll wear him out!—
So thou shalt take thy sweet diurnal feeds—
When he is stuff'd with undigested straw,
Sad food that never visited his jaw!
And staring round him with a brace of beads!

THOMAS HOOD

To Minerva

From The Greek

My temples throb, my pulses boil,
　I'm sick of Song and Ode, and Ballad—
So, Thyrsis, take the Midnight Oil
　And pour it on a lobster salad.

My brain is dull, my sight is foul,
　I cannot write a verse, or read—
Then, Pallas, take away thine Owl,
　And let us have a lark instead.

THOMAS HOOD

Fragment in Imitation of Wordsworth

There is a river clear and fair,
'Tis neither broad nor narrow;
It winds a little here and there—
It winds about like any hare;
And then it takes as straight a course
As on the turnpike road a horse,
　Or through the air an arrow.

The trees that grow upon the shore,
Have grown a hundred years or more;
　So long there is no knowing.
Old Daniel Dobson does not know
When first those trees began to grow;
But still they grew, and grew, and grew,
As if they'd nothing else to do,
　But ever to be growing.

The impulses of air and sky
Have reared their stately stems so high,
   And clothed their boughs with green;
Their leaves the dews of evening quaff,—
   And when the wind blows loud and keen,
I've seen the jolly timbers laugh,
   And shake their sides with merry glee—
   Wagging their heads in mockery.

Fix'd are their feet in solid earth,
   Where winds can never blow;
But visitings of deeper birth
   Have reached their roots below.
For they have gained the river's brink,
And of the living waters drink.

There's little Will, a five years' child—
He is my youngest boy;
To look on eyes so fair and wild,
   It is a very joy:—
He hath conversed with sun and shower,
And dwelt with every idle flower,
   As fresh and gay as them.
He loiters with the briar rose,—
The blue belles are his play-fellows,
   That dance upon their slender stem.

And I have said, my little Will,
Why should not he continue still
   A thing of Nature's rearing?
A thing beyond the world's control—
A living vegetable soul,—
   No human sorrow fearing.

It were a blessed sight to see
That child become a willow tree,
    His brother trees among.
He'd be four time as tall as me,
    And live three times as long.

CATHERINE FANSHAWE

Impromptu

If I were a cassowary
    On the plains of Timbuctoo,
I would eat a missionary,
    Cassock, bands and hymn-book too.

SAMUEL WILBERFORCE

She is Far from the Land

Cables entangling her,
Shipspars for mangling her,
Ropes, sure of strangling her;
Blocks over-dangling her;
Tiller to batter her,
Topmast to shatter her,
Tobacco to spatter her;
Boreas blustering,
Boatswain quite flustering,
Thunder-clouds mustering
To blast her with sulphur—
If the deep don't engulph her;
Sometimes fear's scrutiny
Pries out a mutiny,
Sniffs conflagration,

Or hints at starvation:—
All the sea-dangers,
Buccaneers, rangers,
Pirates and Sallee-men,
Algerine galleymen,
Tornadoes and typhons,
And horrible syphons,
And submarine travels
Thro' roaring sea-navels.
Everything wrong enough,
Long-boat not long enough,
Vessel not strong enough;
Pitch marring frippery,
The deck very slippery,
And the cabin—built sloping,
The Captain a-toping,
And the Mate a blasphemer,
That names his Redeemer,—
With inward uneasiness;
The cook known, by greasiness,
The victuals beslubber'd,
Her bed—in a cupboard;
Things of strange christening,
Snatch'd in her listening,
Blue lights and red lights
And mention of dead-lights,
And shrouds made a theme of,
Things horrid to dream of,—
And *buoys* in the water
To fear all exhort her;
Her friend no Leander,
Herself no sea-gander,
And ne'er a cork jacket
On board of the packet;
The breeze still a stiffening,
The trumpet quite deafening;
Thoughts of repentance,

And doomsday and sentence;
Everything sinister,
Not a church minister,—
Pilot a blunderer,
Coral reefs under her,
Ready to sunder her;
Trunks tipsy-topsy,
The ship in a dropsy;
Waves oversurging her,
Sirens a-dirgeing her;
Sharks all expecting her,
Sword-fish dissecting her,
Crabs with their hand-vices
Punishing land vices;
Sea-dogs and unicorns,
Things with no puny horns,
Mermen carnivorous—
'Good Lord deliver us!'

THOMAS HOOD

from *Melodies*

There was once a young man of Oporta
Who daily got shorter and shorter,
    The reason he said
    Was the hod on his head,
Which was filled with the *heaviest* mortar.

His sister named Lucy O'Finner,
Grew constantly thinner and thinner,
    The reason was plain,
    She slept out in the rain,
And was never allowed any dinner.

LEWIS CARROLL: 1845

93

Brother and Sister

'Sister, sister, go to bed,
Go and rest your weary head,'
Thus the prudent brother said.

'Do you want a battered hide
Or scratches to your face applied?'
Thus the sister calm replied.

'Sister! do not rouse my wrath,
I'd make you into mutton broth
As easily as kill a moth.'

The sister raised her beaming eye,
And looked on him indignantly,
And sternly answered 'Only try!'

Off to the cook he quickly ran,
'Dear cook, pray lend a frying pan
To me, as quickly as you can.'

'And wherefore should I give it you?'
'The reason, cook, is plain to view,
I wish to make an Irish stew.'

'What meat is in that stew to go?'
'My sister'll be the contents.' 'Oh!'
'Will you lend the pan, cook?' 'NO!'

Moral: 'Never stew your sister.'

LEWIS CARROLL

A Visitor

Well, *if* you must know all the facts, I was merely reading a
    pamphlet
When what should I hear at the door but a knock as soft as a
    Zephyr.
I listened and heard it again, so, as loud as I possibly *could* call,
I shouted, 'Don't stand waiting there, come in, let me know
    who you are, sir!'
Mild he entered the room, with his hat in his hand and his
    gloves off,
And a meek gentle bow he performed, while my anger was
    rapidly rising,
'Who *are* you?' I angrily cried, and with hand on his heart as
    he bowed low,
In the gentlest of tones he replied, 'Your servant, Sir
    Pokurranshuvvle.'
Didn't I just ring the bell, 'Here, Tom, Dick, George,
    Andrew!' I bawled out,
'Come here! show this stranger the door!' My summons they
    heard and they did it:
Soon to the door was he guided; once more he turned to me
    and bowed low,
And so, with his hand on his heart, with all possible meekness
    departed.

LEWIS CARROLL

My Fairy

I have a fairy by my side
    Which says I must not sleep,
When once in pain I loudly cried
    It said 'You must not weep.'

If, full of mirth, I smile and grin,
    It says 'You must not laugh,'
When once I wished to drink some gin,
    It said 'You must not quaff.'

When once a meal I wished to taste
    It said 'You must not bite,'
When to the wars I went in haste,
    It said 'You must not fight.'

'What *may* I do?' At length I cried,
    Tired of the painful task,
The fairy quietly replied,
    And said 'You must not ask.'

Moral: 'You mustn't.'

LEWIS CARROLL

A Quotation from Shakespeare with slight improvements

War. Wil't please your grace to go along with us?
P.   No I will sit and watch here by the king.
                             [*Exeunt all but P. H.*]
    'Why doth the crown lie there upon his pillow
    Being so troublesome a bedfellow?
    Oh polished perturbation! golden care!
    That keepst the ports of slumber open wide
    To many a watchful night—sleep with it now!
    Yet not so sound, and half so deeply sweet,
    As he whose brow with homely biggin bound
    Snores out the watch of night.'
K.   Harry I know not
    The meaning of the word you just have used.

P.   What word, my liege?

K.   The word I mean is 'biggin.'

P.   It means a kind of woolen nightcap, sir,
     With which the peasantry are wont to bind
     Their wearied heads, ere that they take their rest.

K.   Thanks for your explanation, pray proceed.

P.   'Snores out the watch of night. Oh majesty!
     When thou dost pinch thy bearer thou dost sit
     Like a rich armour, worn in heat of day
     That scalds with safety.'

K.   Scalding ne'er is safe
     For it produces heat and feverishness
     And blisters on the parched and troubled skin.

P.   Pray interrupt not. 'By his gates of breath
     There lies a downy feather which stirs not.'

K.   I knew not that there was one, brush it off.

P.   'Did he suspire that light and weightless down
     Perforce must move.'

K.   And it *hath* moved already.

P.   It hath *not* moved. 'My gracious lord! my father!
     This sleep is sound indeed, this is a sleep
     That from this golden rigol hath divorced
     So many English—'

K.   What meaneth rigol, Harry?

P.   My liege, I know not, save that it doth enter
     Most apt into the metre.

K.   True, it doth.
     But wherefore use a word which hath no meaning?

P.   My lord, the word is said, for it hath passed
     My lips, and all the powers upon this earth
     Can not unsay it.

K.   You are right, proceed.

P.   'So many English kings; thy due from me
     Is tears and heavy sorrows of the blood
     Which nature, love, and filial tenderness,
     Shall, oh dear father, pay thee plenteously:
     My due from thee is this imperial crown

97

                    Which as—'

K.   'Tis *not* your due, sir! I deny it!

P.   It *is*, my liege! How dare you contradict me?
        Moreover how can you, a sleeper, know
        That which another doth soliloquise?

K.   Your rhetoric is vain, for it is true:
        Therefore no arguments can prove it false.

P.   Yet sure it is not possible, my liege!

K.   Upon its possibility I dwelt not
        I merely said 'twas true.

P.   But yet, my liege,
        What is not possible can never happen,
        Therefore this cannot.

K.   Which do you deny
        That I have heard you or that I'm asleep?

P.   That you're asleep, my liege.

K.   Go on, go on,
        I see you are not fit to reason with.

P.   'Which as immediate from thy place and blood
        Derives itself to me. Lo, here it sits,—
        Which heaven itself shall guard, and put the world's
            whole strength
        Into which giant arm, it shall not force
        This lineal honour from me: this from thee
        Will I to mine leave as 'tis left to me.'

                                        LEWIS CARROLL

Limericks

[1]

There was an Old Man with a beard,
Who said, 'It is just as I feared!—
Two Owls and a Hen, four Larks and a Wren,
Have all built their nests in my beard!'

[2]

There was a Young Person of Crete,
Whose toilette was far from complete;
She dressed in a sack, spickle-speckled with black,
That ombliferous person of Crete.

[3]

There was an Old Man of Madras,
Who rode on a cream-coloured ass;
But the length of its ears, so promoted his fears,
That it killed that Old Man of Madras.

[4]

There was an Old Man in a boat,
Who said, 'I'm afloat! I'm afloat!'
When they said, 'No! you ain't' he was ready to faint,
That unhappy Old Man in a boat.

[5]

There was an old Person whose habits,
Induced him to feed upon Rabbits;
When he'd eaten eighteen, he turned perfectly green,
Upon which he relinquished those habits.

[6]

There was an Old Person of Philæ,
Whose conduct was scroobious and wily;
He rushed up a Palm, when the weather was calm,
And observed all the ruins of Philæ.

EDWARD LEAR: 1846

99

The Palace of Humbug

I dreamt I dwelt in marble halls,
And each damp thing that creeps and crawls
Went wobble-wobble on the walls.

Faint odours of departed cheese,
Blown on the dank, unwholesome breeze,
Awoke the never-ending sneeze.

Strange pictures decked the arras drear,
Strange characters of woe and fear,
The humbugs of the social sphere.

One showed a vain and noisy prig,
That shouted empty words and big
At him that nodded in a wig.

And one, a dotard grim and gray,
Who wasteth childhood's happy day
In work more profitless than play.

Whose icy breast no pity warms,
Whose little victims sit in swarms,
And slowly sob on lower forms.

And one, a green thyme-honoured Bank,
Where flowers are growing wild and rank,
Like weeds that fringe a poisoned tank.

All birds of evil omen there
Flood with rich Notes the tainted air,
The witless wanderer to snare.

The fatal Notes neglected fall,
No creature heeds the treacherous call,
For all those goodly Strawn Baits pall.

The wandering phantom broke and fled,
Straightway I saw within my head
A vision of a ghostly bed,

Where lay two worn decrepit men,
The fictions of a lawyer's pen,
Who never more might breathe again.

The serving-man of Richard Roe
Wept, inarticulate with woe:
She wept, that waited on John Doe.

'Oh rouse,' I urged, 'the waning sense
With tales of tangled evidence,
Of suit, demurrer, and defence.'

'Vain,' she replied, 'such mockeries:
For morbid fancies, such as these,
No suits can suit, no plea can please.'

And bending o'er that man of straw,
She cried in grief and sudden awe,
Not inappropriately, 'Law!'

The well-remembered voice he knew,
He smiled, he faintly muttered 'Sue!'
(Her very name was legal too.)

The night was fled, the dawn was nigh:
A hurricane went raving by,
And swept the Vision from mine eye.

Vanished that dim and ghostly bed,
(The hangings, tape; the tape was red:)
'Tis o'er, and Doe and Roe are dead!

Oh, yet my spirit inly crawls,
What time it shudderingly recalls
That horrid dream of marble halls!

LEWIS CARROLL

She's all my Fancy Painted Him

She's all my fancy painted him
    (I make no idle boast);
If he or you had lost a limb,
    Which would have suffered most?

He said that you had been to her,
    And seen me here before;
But, in another character,
    She was the same of yore.

There was not one that spoke to us,
    Of all that thronged the street:
So he sadly got into a 'bus,
    And pattered with his feet.

They sent him word I had not gone
    (We know it to be true);
If she should push the matter on,
    What would become of you?

They gave her one, they gave me two,
    They gave us three or more;
They all returned from him to you,
    Though they were mine before.

If I or she should chance to be
    Involved in this affair,
He trusts to you to set them free,
    Exactly as we were.

It seemed to me that you had been
    (Before she had this fit)
An obstacle, that came between
    Him, and ourselves, and it.

Don't let him know she liked them best,
    For this must ever be
A secret, kept from all the rest,
    Between yourself and me.

LEWIS CARROLL

[Entrance Exams]

History

1. Draw a historical parallel (after the manner of Plutarch) between Hannibal and Annie Laurie.
2. What internal evidence does the Odyssey afford, that Homer sold his Trojan war-ballads at three yards an obolus?
3. In what way were the shades on the banks of the Styx supplied with spirits?
4. Give a brief account of the Roman Emperors who visited the United States, and state what they did there.
5. Show from the words, 'Hoc erat in votis' (*Sat.* vi., Lib. ii.), that Horace's favourite wine was hock, and that he meant to say 'he always voted for hock.'
6. Draw a parallel between the Children in the Wood and Achilles in the Styx.
7. Name the prima donnas who have appeared in the operas of Virgil and Horace since the 'Virgilii Opera' and 'Horatii Opera' were composed.

Euclid, Arithmetic, and Algebra

1. 'The extremities of a line are points.' Prove this by the rule of railways.
2. Show the fallacy of defining an angle, as 'a worm at one end and a fool at the other.'
3. If one side of a triangle be produced, what is there to prevent the other two sides from also being brought forward?

4. If the gnomon of a sundial be divided into two equal, and also into two unequal parts, what would be its value?
5. If seven horses eat twenty-five acres of grass in three days, what would be their condition on the fourth day? Prove by practice.
6. Reduce two academical years to their lowest terms.

CUTHBERT BEDE

Pop Goes the Weasel!

Up and down the City Road,
  In and out the Eagle,
That's the way the money goes,
  Pop goes the weasel!

A ha'penny for a cotton ball,
  A farthing for a needle,
That's the way the money goes,
  Pop goes the weasel!

Half a pound of tuppenny rice,
  Half a pound of treacle,
Mix it up and make it nice,
  Pop goes the weasel!

Every time my mother goes out,
  The monkey's on the table,
Cracking nuts and eating spice,
  Pop goes the weasel!

If you want to buy a pig,
  Buy a pig with hairs on,
Every hair a penny a pair,
  Pop goes the weasel!

W. R. MARDALE

An Eggstravagance

The Reverend Henry Ward Beecher
Called a hen 'a most elegant creature'.
 The hen, pleased with that.
 Laid two eggs in his hat,
And thus did the hen reward Beecher.

OLIVER WENDELL HOLMES

Intramural Aestivation, or Summer in Town, by a Teacher of Latin

In candent ire the solar splendor flames;
The foles, languescent, pend from arid rames;
His humid front the cive, anheling, wipes,
And dreams of erring on ventiferous ripes.

How dulce to vive occult to mortal eyes,
Dorm on the herb with none to supervise,
Carp the suave berries from the crescent vine,
And bibe the flow from longicaudate kine!

To me, alas! no verdurous visions come,
Save yon exiguous pool's conferva-scum,—
No concave vast repeats the tender hue
That laves my milk-jug with celestial blue!

Me wretched! Let me curr to quercine shades!
Effund your albid hausts, lactiferous maids!
O, might I vole to some umbrageous clump,—
Depart,—be off,—excede,—evade,—erump!

OLIVER WENDELL HOLMES

Limericks

1

There was an old person of Dover,
Who rushed through a field of blue Clover;
But some very large bees, stung his nose and his knees,
So he very soon went back to Dover.

2

There was an Old Man of Vesuvius,
Who studied the works of Vitruvius;
When the flames burnt his book, to drinking he took,
That morbid Old Man of Vesuvius.

3

There was an Old Man of Dundee,
Who frequented the top of a tree;
When disturbed by the crows, he abruptly arose,
And exclaimed, 'I'll return to Dundee.'

4

There was an old person of Hove,
Who frequented the depths of a grove;
Where he studied his books, with the wrens and the rooks,
That tranquil old person of Hove.

5

There was an old man of Three Bridges,
Whose mind was distracted by midges,
He sate on a wheel, eating underdone veal,
Which relieved that old man of Three Bridges.

EDWARD LEAR

A Letter to Evelyn Baring

Thrippsy pillivinx,
>   Inky tinky pobbleboskle abblesquabs?—
Flosky! beebul trimble flosky!—Okul
scratchabibblebongibo, viddle squibble tog-a-tog,
ferrymoyassity amsky flamsky ramsky damsky
crocklefether squiggs.

>   Flinkywisty pomm,
>   Slushypipp
>   EDWARD LEAR

>   She sits upon her Bulbul
>   Through the long long hours of night—
>   And o'er the dark horizon gleams
>   The Yashmack's fitful light.
>   The lone Yaourt sails slowly down
>   The deep and craggy dell—
>   And from his lofty nest, loud screams
>   The white plumed Asphodel.

>   EDWARD LEAR

Ballad

The auld wife sat at her ivied door,
>   (*Butter and eggs and a pound of cheese*)
A thing she had frequently done before;
>   And her spectacles lay on her apron'd knees.

The piper he piped on the hill-top high,
>   (*Butter and eggs and a pound of cheese*)

Till the cow said 'I die,' and the goose ask'd 'Why?'
    And the dog said nothing, but search'd for fleas.

The farmer he strode through the square farmyard;
    (*Butter and eggs and a pound of cheese*)
His last brew of ale was a trifle hard—
    The connexion of which with the plot one sees.

The farmer's daughter hath frank blue eyes;
    (*Butter and eggs and a pound of cheese*)
She hears the rooks caw in the windy skies,
    As she sits at her lattice and shells her peas.

The farmer's daughter hath ripe red lips;
    (*Butter and eggs and a pound of cheese*)
If you try to approach her, away she skips
    Over tables and chairs with apparent ease.

The farmer's daughter hath soft brown hair
    (*Butter and eggs and a pound of cheese*)
And I met with a ballad, I can't say where,
    Which wholly consisted of lines like these.

Part II

She sat with her hands 'neath her dimpled cheeks,
    (*Butter and eggs and a pound of cheese*)
And spake not a word. While a lady speaks
    There is hope, but she didn't even sneeze.

She sat, with her hands 'neath her crimson cheeks;
    (*Butter and eggs and a pound of cheese*)
She gave up mending her father's breeks,
    And let the cat roll in her new chemise.

She sat, with her hands 'neath her burning cheeks,
    (*Butter and eggs and a pound of cheese*)

And gazed at the piper for thirteen weeks;
  Then she follow'd him out o'er the misty leas.

Her sheep follow'd her, as their tails did them.
  (*Butter and eggs and a pound of cheese*)
And this song is consider'd a perfect gem,
  And as to the meaning, it's what you please.

C. S. CALVERLEY

The Cock and the Bull

You see this pebble-stone? It's a thing I bought
Of a bit of a chit of a boy i' the mid o' the day—
I like to dock the smaller parts-o'-speech,
As we curtail the already cur-tail'd cur
(You catch the paronomasia, play 'po' words?)
Did, rather, i' the pre-Landseerian days.
Well, to my muttons. I purchased the concern,
And clapt it i' my poke, having given for same
By way o' chop, swop, barter or exchange—
'Chop' was my snickering dandiprat's own term—
One shilling and fourpence, current coin o' the realm.
O-n-e one and f-o-u-r four
Pence, one and fourpence—you are with me, sir?—
What hour it skills not: ten or eleven o' the clock,
One day (and what a roaring day it was
Go shop or sight-see—bar a spit o' rain!)
In February, eighteen sixty nine,
Alexandrina Victoria, Fidei
Hm—hm—how runs the jargon? being on throne.

  Such, sir, are all the facts, succinctly put,
The basis or substratum—what you will—
Of the impending eighty thousand lines.

'Not much in 'em either,' quoth perhaps simple Hodge.
But there's a superstructure. Wait a bit.

Mark first the rationale of the thing:
Hear logic rivel and levigate the deed.
That shilling—and for matter o' that, the pence—
I had o' course upo' me—wi' me say—
(*Mecum*'s the Latin, make a note o' that)
When I popp'd pen i' stand, scratch'd ear, wiped snout,
(Let everybody wipe his own himself)
Sniff'd—tch!—at snuffbox; tumbled up, he-heed,
Haw-haw'd (not hee-haw'd, that's another guess thing:)
Then fumbled at, and stumbled out of, door,
I shoved the timber ope wi' my omoplat;
And *in vestibulo*, i' the lobby to-wit,
(Iacobi Facciolati's rendering, sir,)
Donn'd galligaskins, antigropeloes,
And so forth; and, complete with hat and gloves,
One on and one a-dangle i' my hand,
And ombrifuge (Lord love you!), case o' rain,
I flopp'd forth, 'sbuddikins! on my own ten toes,
(I do assure you there be ten of them),
And went clump-clumping up hill and down dale
To find myself o' the sudden i' front o' the boy.
But case I hadn't 'em on me, could I ha' bought
This sort-o'-kind-o'-what-you-might-call toy,
This pebble-thing, o' the boy-thing? Q. E. D.
That's proven without aid from mumping Pope,
Sleek porporate or bloated Cardinal.
(Isn't it, old Fatchaps? You're in Euclid now.)
So, having the shilling—having i' fact a lot—
And pence and halfpence, ever so many o' them,
I purchased, as I think I said before,
The pebble (*lapis, lapidis, -di, -dem, -de*—
What nouns 'crease short i' the genitive, Fatchaps, eh?)
O' the boy, a bare-legg'd beggarly son of a gun,
For one-and-fourpence. Here we are again.

Now Law steps in, bigwigg'd, voluminous-jaw'd;
Investigates and re-investigates.
Was the transaction illegal? Law shakes head.
Perpend, sir, all the bearings of the case.

At first the coin was mine, the chattel his.
But now (by virtue of the said exchange
And barter) *vice versa* all the coin,
Per juris operationem, vests
I' the boy and his assigns till ding o' doom;
(*In sæcula sæculo-o-o-orum;*
I think I hear the Abate mouth out that.)
To have and hold the same to him and them.

Confer some idiot on Conveyancing.
Whereas the pebble and every part thereof,
And all that appertaineth thereunto,
Quodcunque pertinet ad eam rem,
(I fancy, sir, my Latin's rather pat)
Or shall, will, may, might, can, could, would or should,
(*Subaudi cætera*—clap we to the close—
For what's the good of law in a case o' the kind)
Is mine to all intents and purposes.
This settled, I resume the thread o' the tale.

Now for a touch o' the vendor's quality.
He says a gen'lman bought a pebble of him,
(This pebble i' sooth, sir, which I hold i' my hand)—
And paid for't, *like* a gen'lman, on the nail.
'Did I o'ercharge him a ha'penny? Devil a bit.
Fiddlepin's end! Get out, you blazing ass!
Gabble o' the goose. Don't bugaboo-baby *me!*
Go double or quits? Yah! tittup! what's the odds?'
—There's the transaction view'd i' the vendor's light.

Next ask that dumpled hag, stood snuffling by,
With her three frowsy blowsy brats o' babes,

The scum o' the kennel, cream o' the filth-heap—Faugh!
Aie, aie, aie, aie! ὀτοτοτοτοῖ,
('Stead which we blurt out Hoighty toighty now)—
And the baker and candlestickmaker, and Jack and Gill,
Blear'd Goody this and queasy Gaffer that.
Ask the schoolmaster. Take schoolmaster first.

He saw a gentleman purchase of a lad
A stone, and pay for it *rite*, on the square,
And carry it off *per saltum*, jauntily,
Propria quæ maribus, gentleman's property now
(Agreeably to the law explain'd above),
In proprium usum, for his private ends.
The boy he chuck'd a brown i' the air, and bit
I' the face the shilling: heaved a thumping stone
At a lean hen that ran cluck clucking by,
(And hit her, dead as nail i' post o' door,)
Then *abiit*—what's the Ciceronian phrase?—
Excessit, evasit, erupit—off slogs boy;
Off like bird, *avi similis*—(you observed
The dative? Pretty i' the Mantuan!)—*Anglice*
Off in three flea skips. *Hactenus, so far*,
So good, *tam bene. Bene, satis, male*—,
Where was I with my trope 'bout one in a quag?
I did once hitch the syntax into verse:
Verbum personale, a verb personal,
Concordat—ay, 'agrees,' old Fatchaps—*cum
Nominativo*, with its nominative,
Genere, i' point o' gender, *numero*,
O' number, *et persona*, and person. *Ut*,
Instance: *Sol ruit*, down flops sun, *et* and,
Montes umbrantur, out flounce mountains. Pah!
Excuse me, sir, I think I'm going mad.
You see the trick on't though, and can yourself
Continue the discourse *ad libitum*.
It takes up about eighty thousand lines,
A thing imagination boggles at:

And might, odds-bobs, sir! in judicious hands,
Extend from here to Mesopotamy.

C. S. CALVERLEY

How Doth . . .

How doth the little crocodile
    Improve his shining tail,
And pour the waters of the Nile
    On every golden scale!

How cheerfully he seems to grin,
    How neatly spreads his claws,
And welcomes little fishes in
    With gently smiling jaws!

LEWIS CARROLL

Father William

'You are old, Father William,' the young man said,
    'And your hair has become very white;
And yet you incessantly stand on your head—
    Do you think, at your age, it is right?'

'In my youth,' Father William replied to his son,
    'I feared it might injure the brain;
But, now that I'm perfectly sure I have none,
    Why, I do it again and again.'

'You are old,' said the youth, 'as I mentioned before,
    And have grown most uncommonly fat;
Yet you turned a back-somersault in at the door—
    Pray, what is the reason of that?'

'In my youth,' said the sage, as he shook his grey locks,
    'I kept all my limbs very supple
By the use of this ointment—one shilling the box—
    Allow me to sell you a couple?'

'You are old,' said the youth, 'and your jaws are too weak
    For anything tougher than suet;
Yet you finished the goose, with the bones and the beak—
    Pray, how did you manage to do it?'

'In my youth,' said his father, 'I took to the law,
    And argued each case with my wife;
And the muscular strength, which it gave to my jaw,
    Has lasted the rest of my life.'

'You are old,' said the youth, 'one would hardly suppose
    That your eye was as steady as ever;
Yet you balanced an eel on the end of your nose—
    What made you so awfully clever?'

'I have answered three questions, and that is enough,'
    Said his father; 'don't give yourself airs!
Do you think I can listen all day to such stuff?
    Be off, or I'll kick you down stairs!'

LEWIS CARROLL

The Mad Hatter's Song

Twinkle, twinkle, little bat!
How I wonder what you're at!
Up above the world you fly,
Like a tea-tray in the sky.
            Twinkle, twinkle—

LEWIS CARROLL

The Mouse's Tale

Fury said to a
    mouse, That he
      met in the
        house,
          'Let us
           both go to
           law: *I* will
          prosecute
          you. Come,
         I'll take no
        denial; We
       must have a
      trial: For
    really this
    morning I've
  nothing
to do.'
  Said the
    mouse to the
    cur, 'Such
    a trial,
      dear Sir,
      With
        no jury
          or judge,
           would be
          wasting
        our
        breath.'
      'I'll be
     judge, I'll
    be jury,'
  Said
  cunning
  old Fury:
  'I'll
    try the
      whole
      cause,
    and
    condemn
    you
  to
 death.'

LEWIS CARROLL

Evidence Read at the Trial of the Knave of Hearts

They told me you had been to her,
   And mentioned me to him:
She gave me a good character,
   But said I could not swim.

He sent them word I had not gone,
   (We know it to be true):
If she should push the matter on,
   What would become of you?

I gave her one, they gave him two,
   You gave us three or more;
They all returned from him to you,
   Though they were mine before.

If I or she should chance to be
   Involved in this affair,
He trusts to you to set them free,
   Exactly as we were.

My notion was that you had been
   (Before she had this fit)
An obstacle that came between
   Him, and ourselves, and it.

Don't let him know she liked them best,
   For this must ever be
A secret kept from all the rest,
   Between yourself and me.

LEWIS CARROLL

The Duchess's Lullaby

Speak roughly to your little boy,
   And beat him when he sneezes:
He only does it to annoy,
   Because he knows it teases.

Wow! wow! wow!

I speak severely to my boy,
   I beat him when he sneezes;
For he can thoroughly enjoy
   The pepper when he pleases!

Wow! wow! wow!

LEWIS CARROLL

Alice's Recitation

'Tis the voice of the Lobster; I heard him declare,
'You have baked me too brown, I must sugar my hair.'
As a duck with its eyelids, so he with his nose
Trims his belt and his buttons, and turns out his toes.
When the sands are all dry, he is gay as a lark,
And will talk in contemptuous tones of the Shark:
But, when the tide rises and sharks are around,
His voice has a timid and tremulous sound.

I passed by his garden, and marked, with one eye,
How the Owl and the Panther were sharing a pie:
The Panther took pie-crust, and gravy, and meat,
While the Owl had the dish as its share of the treat.

When the pie was all finished, the Owl, as a boon,
Was kindly permitted to pocket the spoon:
But the Panther obtained both the fork and the knife,
So, when *he* lost his temper, the Owl lost its life.

LEWIS CARROLL

Turtle Soup

Beautiful Soup, so rich and green,
Waiting in a hot tureen!
Who for such dainties would not stoop?
Soup of the evening, beautiful Soup!
Soup of the evening, beautiful Soup!
    Beau—ootiful Soo—oop!
    Beau—ootiful Soo—oop!
Soo—oop of the e—e—evening,
    Beautiful, beautiful Soup!

Beautiful Soup! Who cares for fish,
Game, or any other dish?
Who would not give all else for two p
ennyworth only of beautiful Soup?
Pennyworth only of beautiful Soup?
    Beau—ootiful Soo—oop!
    Beau—ootiful Soo—oop!
Soo—oop of the e—e—evening,
    Beautiful, beauti—FUL SOUP!

LEWIS CARROLL

The Mock Turtle's Song

'Will you walk a little faster?' said a whiting to a snail.
'There's a porpoise close behind us, and he's treading on my
  tail.
See how eagerly the lobsters and the turtles all advance!
They are waiting on the shingle—will you come and join the
  dance?
  Will you, won't you, will you, won't you, will you join
    the dance?
  Will you, won't you, will you, won't you, won't you
    join the dance?

'You can really have no notion how delightful it will be,
When they take us up and throw us, with the lobsters, out
  to sea!'
But the snail replied 'Too far, too far!' and gave a look
  askance—
Said he thanked the whiting kindly, but he would not join
  the dance.
  Would not, could not, would not, could not, would not
    join the dance.
  Would not, could not, would not, could not, could not
    join the dance.

'What matters it how far we go?' his scaly friend replied.
'There is another shore, you know, upon the other side.
The further off from England the nearer is to France—
Then turn not pale, beloved snail, but come and join the
  dance.
  Will you, won't you, will you, won't you, will you join
    the dance?
  Will you, won't you, will you, won't you, won't you join
    the dance?'

LEWIS CARROLL

119

Eclogue

Composed at Cannes, December 9th, 1867

Interlocutors—MR. LEAR AND MR. AND MRS. SYMONDS

Edwardus.—What makes you look so black, so glum, so cross?
Is it neuralgia, headache, or remorse?

Johannes.—What makes you look as cross, or even more so?
Less like a man than is a broken Torso?

E.—What if my life is odious, should I grin?
If you are savage, need I care a pin?

J.—And if I suffer, am I then an owl?
May I not frown and grind my teeth and growl?

E.—Of course you may; but may not I growl too?
May I not frown and grind my teeth like you?

J.—See Catherine comes! To her, to her,
Let each his several miseries refer;
She shall decide whose woes are least or worst,
And which, as growler, shall rank last or first.

Catherine.—Proceed to growl, in silence I'll attend,
And hear your foolish growlings to the end;
And when they're done, I shall correctly judge
Which of your griefs are real or only fudge.
Begin, let each his mournful voice prepare,
(And, pray, however angry, do not swear!)

J.—We came abroad for warmth, and find sharp cold!
Cannes is an imposition, and we're sold.

E.—Why did I leave my native land, to find
Sharp hailstones, snow, and most disgusting wind?

J.—What boots it that we orange trees or lemons see,
   If we must suffer from *such* vile inclemency?

E.—Why did I take the lodgings I have got,
   Where all I don't want is:—all I want not?

J.—Last week I called aloud, O! O! O! O!
   The ground is wholly overspread with snow!
   Is that at any rate a theme for mirth
   Which makes a sugar-cake of all the earth?

E.—Why must I sneeze and snuffle, groan and cough,
   If my hat's on my head, or if it's off?
   Why must I sink all poetry in this prose,
   The everlasting blowing of my nose?

J.—When I walk out the mud my footsteps clogs,
   Besides, I suffer from attacks of dogs.

E.—Me a vast awful bulldog, black and brown,
   Completely terrified when near the town;
   As calves, perceiving butchers, trembling reel,
   So did *my* calves the approaching monster feel.

J.—Already from two rooms we're driven away,
   Because the beastly chimneys smoke all day:
   Is this a trifle, say? Is this a joke?
   That we, like hams, should be becooked in smoke?

E.—Say! what avails it that my servant speaks
   Italian, English, Arabic, and Greek,
   Besides Albanian: if he don't speak French,
   How can he ask for salt, or shrimps, or tench?

J.—When on the foolish hearth fresh wood I place,
   It whistles, sings, and squeaks, before my face:
   And if it does unless the fire burns bright,
   And if it does, yet squeaks, how can I write?

E.—Alas! I needs must go and call on swells,
    That they may say, 'Pray draw me the Estrelles.'
    On one I went last week to leave a card,
    The swell was out—the servant eyed me hard:
    'This chap's a thief disguised,' his face expressed:
    If I go there again, may I be blest!

J.—Why must I suffer in this wind and gloom?
    Roomattics in a vile cold attic room?

E.—Swells drive about the road with haste and fury,
    As Jehu drove about all over Jewry.
    Just now, while walking slowly, I was all but
    Run over by the Lady Emma Talbot,
    Whom not long since a lovely babe I knew,
    With eyes and cap-ribbons of perfect blue.

J.—Downstairs and upstairs, every blessed minute,
    There's each room with pianofortes in it.
    How can I write with noises such as those?
    And, being always discomposed, compose?

E.—Seven Germans through my garden lately strayed,
    And all on instruments of torture played;
  ‘ They blew, they screamed, they yelled: how can I
        paint
    Unless my room is quiet, which it ain't?

J.—How can I study if a hundred flies
    Each moment blunder into both my eyes?

E.—How can I draw with green or blue or red,
    If flies and beetles vex my old bald head?

J.—How can I translate German Metaphys-
    Ics, if mosquitoes round my forehead whizz?

E.—I've bought some bacon, (though it's much too fat,)
    But round the house there prowls a hideous cat:
    Once should I see my bacon in her mouth,
    What care I if my rooms look north or south?

J.—Pain from a pane in one cracked window comes,
    Which sings and whistles, buzzes, shrieks and
        hums;
    In vain amain with pain the pane with this chord
    I fain would strain to stop the beastly *dis*cord!

E.—If rain and wind and snow and such like ills
    Continue here, how shall I pay my bills?
    For who through cold and slush and rain will come
    To see my drawings and to purchase some?
    And if they don't, what destiny is mine?
    How can I ever get to Palestine?

J.—The blinding sun strikes through the olive trees,
    When I walk out, and always makes me sneeze.

E.—Next door, if all night long the moon is shining,
    There sits a dog, who wakes me up with whining.
Cath.—Forbear! You both are bores, you've growled
      enough:
    No longer will I listen to such stuff!
    All men have nuisances and bores to afflict 'um:
    Hark then, and bow to my official dictum!
    For you, Johannes, there is most excuse,
    (Some interruptions are the very deuce,)
    You're younger than the other cove, who surely
    Might have some sense—besides, you're somewhat
      poorly.
    This therefore is my sentence, that you nurse
    The Baby for seven hours, and nothing worse.
    For you, Edwardus, I shall say no more
    Than that your griefs are fudge, yourself a bore:

Return at once to cold, stewed, minced, hashed
    mutton—
To wristbands ever guiltless of a button—
To raging winds and sea, (where don't you wish
Your luck may ever let you catch one fish?)—
To make large drawings nobody will buy—
To paint oil pictures which will never dry—
To write new books which nobody will read—
To drink weak tea, on tough old pigs to feed—
Till spring-time brings the birds and leaves and
    flowers,
And time restores a world of happier hours.

EDWARD LEAR

[The Cannibals' Grace before Meat]

(Sung by the savages as they danced round the Latin
grammar master, in a hamper with his head shaved, while
two savages floured him, before putting him to the fire to
be cooked)

Choo a choo a choo tooth.
    Muntch, muntch. Nycey!
Choo a choo a choo tooth.
    Muntch, muntch. Nycey!

CHARLES DICKENS

Foreign Literature

To the Editor of the National Standard

Sir,

I was much pleased with the following pretty
pastoral in the Breton dialect, which I found lately
in some numbers of the French Literary Journal ...

W.

> Choeses me boue er plach yoang,
>   Hi e garau perpet,
> Mas helas! me halon paûr
>   Hi des me zileset.
>
> Pi greden en em hare,
>   Contant oue me halon,
> Bourmen he don didrompet
>   Ia gole glaharet on.
>
> Na me chahuet me'en, doucic,
>   Ne zelet quit do'heign;
> Zel er haranté tromp lus
>   Ne de quet ehiu teign.
>
> Ma me guelet m'en, doucic,
>   Ha pe veign me hunon;
> Dahlet hon comzan gwen oh
>   Drouc e rand dem halon.
>
> Ha pe glehuan en druhumel
>   Da geneign ar er bar;
> Me lar gahus e li halon,
>   Neh quet pel doh hi far.
>
> Ha re veign marhue, doucic,
>   Hui lareign ar me be,
> Che tu be en deu yoang
>   Marhue quet carante!

W. M. THACKERAY: 1833

125

A 'Prize' Poem

Full many a gem of purest ray serene,
That to be hated needs but to be seen,
Invites my lays; be present sylvan maids,
And graceful deer reposing in the shades.

I am the Morning and the Evening Star,
Drag the slow barge, or wheel the rapid car,
While wrapped in fire the realms of ether glow.
Or private dirt in public virtue throw.

How small of all that human hearts endure
The short and simple annals of the poor!
I would commend their bodies to the rack;
At least we'll die with harness on our back!

Remote, unfriended, melancholy, slow,
Virtue alone is happiness below:
As vipers sting, though dead, by some review;
And now thou seest my soul's angelic hue.

SHIRLEY BROOKS

New Proverb

Early to bed and early to rise
Is the way to feel stupid and have red eyes.

SHIRLEY BROOKS

What's your name?
Pudden Tame.
What's your other?

Bread and Butter.
Where do you live?
In a sieve.
What's your number?
Cucumber.

ANON

Poeta Fit, non Nascitur

'How shall I be a poet?
  How shall I write in rhyme:
You told me once 'the very wish
  Partook of the sublime.'
Then tell me how! Don't put me off
  With your "another time"!'

The old man smiled to see him,
  To hear his sudden sally;
He liked the lad to speak his mind
  Enthusiastically;
And thought 'There's no hum-drum in him,
  Nor any shilly-shally.'

'And would you be a poet
  Before you've been to school?
Ah, well! I hardly thought you
  So absolute a fool.
First learn to be spasmodic—
  A very simple rule.

'For first you write a sentence,
  And then you chop it small;
Then mix the bits, and sort them out
  Just as they chance to fall:
The order of the phrases makes
  No difference at all.

127

'Then, if you'd be impressive,
    Remember what I say,
That abstract qualities begin
    With capitals alway:
The True, the Good, the Beautiful—
    Those are the things that pay!

'Next, when you are describing
    A shape, or sound, or tint;
Don't state the matter plainly,
    But put it in a hint;
And learn to look at all things
    With a sort of mental squint.'

'For instance, if I wished, Sir,
    Of mutton-pies to tell,
Should I say "dreams of fleecy flocks
Pent in a wheaten cell"?'
'Why, yes,' the old man said: 'that phrase
Would answer very well.

'Then fourthly, there are epithets
    That suit with any word—
As well as Harvey's Reading Sauce
    With fish, or flesh, or bird—
Of these, "wild," "lonely," "weary," "strange,"
    Are much to be preferred.'

'And will it do, O will it do
    To take them in a lump—
As "the wild man went his weary way
    To a strange and lonely pump"?'
'Nay, nay! You must not hastily
    To such conclusions jump.

'Such epithets, like pepper,
    Give zest to what you write;

And, if you strew them sparely,
    They whet the appetite:
But if you lay them on too thick,
    You spoil the matter quite!

'Last, as to the arrangement:
    Your reader, you should show him.
Must take what information he
    Can get, and look for no im-
mature disclosure of the drift
    And purpose of your poem.

'Therefore, to test his patience—
    How much he can endure—
Mention no places, names, or dates,
    And evermore be sure
Throughout the poem to be found
    Consistently obscure.

'First fix upon the limit
    To which it shall extend:
Then fill it up with "Padding"
    (Beg some of any friend):
Your great SENSATION-STANZA
    You place towards the end.'

'And what is a Sensation,
    Grandfather, tell me, pray?
I think I never heard the word
    So used before to-day:
Be kind enough to mention one
    "Exempli gratiâ." '

And the old man, looking sadly
    Across the garden-lawn,
Where here and there a dew-drop
    Yet glittered in the dawn,

Said 'Go to the Adelphi,
   And see the "Colleen Bawn."'

'The word is due to Boucicault—
   The theory is his,
Where Life becomes a Spasm,
   And History a Whiz:
If that is not Sensation,
   I don't know what it is.

'Now try your hand, ere Fancy
   Have lost its present glow——'
'And then,' his grandson added,
   'We'll publish it, you know:
Green cloth—gold-lettered at the back—
   In duodecimo!'

Then proudly smiled that old man
   To see the eager lad
Rush madly for his pen and ink
   And for his blotting-pad—
But, when he thought of *publishing*,
   His face grew stern and sad.

LEWIS CARROLL

Tèma con Variazióni

[Why is it that Poetry has never yet been subjected to that process
of Dilution which has proved so advantageous to her sister-art
Music? The Diluter gives us first a few notes of some well-known
Air, then a dozen bars of his own, then a few more notes of the
Air, and so on alternately: thus saving the listener, if not from all
risk of recognising the melody at all, at least from the too-exciting
transports which it might produce in a more concentrated form.
The process is termed 'setting' by Composers, and any one, that

has ever experienced the emotion of being unexpectedly set down in a heap of mortar, will recognise the truthfulness of this happy phrase.

For truly, just as the genuine Epicure lingers lovingly over a morsel of supreme Venison—whose every fibre seems to murmur 'Excelsior!'—yet swallows, ere returning to the toothsome dainty, great mouthfuls of oatmeal-porridge and winkles: and just as the perfect Connoisseur in Claret permits himself but one delicate sip, and then tosses off a pint or more of boarding-school beer: so also——]

> I never loved a dear Gazelle—
>   Nor anything that cost me much:
> High prices profit those who sell,
>   But why should I be fond of such?
>
> To glad me with his soft black eye
>   My son comes trotting home from school;
> He's had a fight but can't tell why—
>   He always was a little fool!
>
> But, when he came to know me well,
>   He kicked me out, her testy Sire:
> And when I stained my hair, that Belle
>   Might note the change, and thus admire
>
> And love me, it was sure to dye
>   A muddy green, or staring blue:
> Whilst one might trace, with half an eye,
>   The still triumphant carrot through.

LEWIS CARROLL

The White Knight's Ballad

I'll tell thee everything I can;
   There's little to relate.
I saw an aged aged man,
   A-sitting on a gate.
'Who are you, aged man?' I said.
   'And how is it you live?'
And his answer trickled through my head
   Like water through a sieve.

He said 'I look for butterflies
   That sleep among the wheat:
I make them into mutton-pies,
   And sell them in the street.
I sell them unto men,' he said,
   'Who sail on stormy seas;
And that's the way I get my bread—
   A trifle, if you please.'

But I was thinking of a plan
   To dye one's whiskers green,
And always use so large a fan
   That they could not be seen.
So, having no reply to give
   To what the old man said,
I cried 'Come, tell me how you live!'
   And thumped him on the head.

His accents mild took up the tale:
   He said 'I go my ways,
And when I find a mountain-rill,
   I set it in a blaze;
And thence they make a stuff they call
   Rowland's Macassar Oil—

Yet twopence-halfpenny is all
  They give me for my toil.'

But I was thinking of a way
  To feed oneself on batter,
And so go on from day to day
  Getting a little fatter.
I shook him well from side to side,
  Until his face was blue:
'Come, tell me how you live,' I cried
  'And what it is you do!'

He said 'I hunt for haddocks' eyes
  Among the heather bright,
And work them into waistcoat-buttons
  In the silent night.
And these I do not sell for gold
  Or coin of silvery shine,
But for a copper halfpenny,
  And that will purchase nine.

'I sometimes dig for buttered rolls,
  Or set limed twigs for crabs;
I sometimes search the grassy knolls
  For wheels of hansom-cabs.
And that's the way' (he gave a wink)
  'By which I get my wealth—
And very gladly will I drink
  Your Honour's noble health.'

I heard him then, for I had just
  Completed my design
To keep the Menai bridge from rust
  By boiling it in wine.
I thanked him much for telling me
  The way he got his wealth.
But chiefly for his wish that he
  Might drink my noble health.

And now, if e'er by chance I put
　　My fingers into glue,
Or madly squeeze a right-hand foot
　　Into a left-hand shoe
Or if I drop upon my toe
　　A very heavy weight,
I weep, for it reminds me so
Of that old man I used to know—
Whose look was mild, whose speech was slow,
Whose hair was whiter than the snow,
Whose face was very like a crow,
With eyes, like cinders, all aglow,
Who seemed distracted with his woe,
Who rocked his body to and fro,
And muttered mumblingly and low,
As if his mouth were full of dough,
Who snorted like a buffalo—
That summer evening long ago
　　A-sitting on a gate.

LEWIS CARROLL

Jabberwocky

'Twas brillig, and the slithy toves
　　Did gyre and gimble in the wabe;
All mimsy were the borogoves,
　　And the mome raths outgrabe.

'Beware the Jabberwock, my son!
　　The jaws that bite, the claws that catch!
Beware the Jubjub bird, and shun
　　The frumious Bandersnatch!'

He took his vorpal sword in hand:
　　Long time the manxome foe he sought—

So rested he by the Tumtum tree,
    And stood awhile in thought.

And as in uffish thought he stood,
    The Jabberwock, with eyes of flame,
Came whiffling through the tulgey wood,
    And burbled as it came!

One, two! One, two! And through and through
    The vorpal blade went snicker-snack!
He left it dead, and with its head
    He went galumphing back.

'And hast thou slain the Jabberwock?
    Come to my arms, my beamish boy!
O frabjous day! Callooh! Callay!'
    He chortled in his joy.

'Twas brillig, and the slithy toves
    Did gyre and gimble in the wabe;
All mimsy were the borogoves,
    And the mome raths outgrabe.

                                        LEWIS CARROLL

Humpty Dumpty's Recitation

In winter, when the fields are white,
I sing this song for your delight——

In spring, when woods are getting green,
I'll try and tell you what I mean.

In summer, when the days are long,
Perhaps you'll understand the song:

In autumn, when the leaves are brown,
Take pen and ink, and write it down.

I sent a message to the fish:
I told them 'This is what I wish.'

The little fishes of the sea,
They sent an answer back to me.

The little fishes' answer was
'We cannot do it, Sir, because——'

I sent to them again to say
'It will be better to obey.'

The fishes answered with a grin,
'Why, what a temper you are in!'

I told them once, I told them twice:
They would not listen to advice.

I took a kettle large and new,
Fit for the deed I had to do.

My heart went hop, my heart went thump;
I filled the kettle at the pump.

Then someone came to me and said
'The little fishes are in bed.'

I said to him, I said it plain,
'Then you must wake them up again.'

I said it very loud and clear;
I went and shouted in his ear.

But he was very stiff and proud;
He said 'You needn't shout so loud!'

And he was very proud and stiff;
He said 'I'd go and wake them, if——'

I took a corkscrew from the shelf:
I went to wake them up myself.

And when I found the door was locked,
I pulled and pushed and kicked and knocked.

And when I found the door was shut,
I tried to turn the handle, but——

LEWIS CARROLL

\<The Wasp's Song\>

When I was young, my ringlets waved
    And curled and crinkled on my head:
And then they said 'You should be shaved,
    And wear a yellow wig instead.'

But when I followed their advice,
    And they had noticed the effect,
They said I did not look so nice
    As they had ventured to expect.

They said it did not fit, and so
    It made me look extremely plain:
But what was I to do, you know?
    My ringlets would not grow again.

So now that I am old and gray,
    And all my hair is nearly gone,
They take my wig from me and say
    'How can you put such rubbish on?'

And still, whenever I appear,
   They hoot at me and call me 'Pig!'
And that is why they do it, dear,
   Because I wear a yellow wig.

LEWIS CARROLL

The Walrus and the Carpenter

The sun was shining on the sea,
   Shining with all his might:
He did his very best to make
   The billows smooth and bright—
And this was odd, because it was
   The middle of the night.

The moon was shining sulkily,
   Because she thought the sun
Had got no business to be there
   After the day was done—
'It's very rude of him,' she said,
   'To come and spoil the fun!'

The sea was wet as wet could be,
   The sands were dry as dry.
You could not see a cloud, because
   No cloud was in the sky:
No birds were flying overhead—
   There were no birds to fly.

The Walrus and the Carpenter
   Were walking close at hand;
They wept like anything to see
   Such quantities of sand:
'If this were only cleared away,'
   They said, 'it *would* be grand!'

'If seven maids with seven mops
  Swept it for half a year,
Do you suppose,' the Walrus said,
  'That they could get it clear?'
'I doubt it,' said the Carpenter,
  And shed a bitter tear.

'O Oysters, come and walk with us!'
  The Walrus did beseech.
'A pleasant walk, a pleasant talk,
  Along the briny beach:
We cannot do with more than four,
  To give a hand to each.'

The eldest Oyster looked at him,
  But never a word he said:
The eldest Oyster winked his eye,
  And shook his heavy head—
Meaning to say he did not choose
  To leave the oyster-bed.

But four young Oysters hurried up,
  All eager for the treat:
Their coats were brushed, their faces washed,
  Their shoes were clean and neat—
And this was odd, because, you know,
  They hadn't any feet.

Four other Oysters followed them,
  And yet another four;
And thick and fast they came at last,
  And more, and more, and more—
All hopping through the frothy waves,
  And scrambling to the shore.

The Walrus and the Carpenter
  Walked on a mile or so,

And then they rested on a rock
  Conveniently low:
And all the little Oysters stood
  And waited in a row.

'The time has come,' the Walrus said,
  'To talk of many things:
Of shoes—and ships—and sealing-wax—
  Of cabbages—and kings—
And why the sea is boiling hot—
  And whether pigs have wings.'

'But wait a bit,' the Oysters cried,
  'Before we have our chat;
For some of us are out of breath,
  And all of us are fat!'
'No hurry!' said the Carpenter.
  They thanked him much for that.

'A loaf of bread,' the Walrus said,
  'Is what we chiefly need:
Pepper and vinegar besides
  Are very good indeed—
Now if you're ready, Oysters dear,
  We can begin to feed.'

'But not on us!' the Oysters cried,
  Turning a little blue.
'After such kindness, that would be
  A dismal thing to do!'
'The night is fine,' the Walrus said.
  'Do you admire the view?'

'It was so kind of you to come!
  And you are very nice!'
The Carpenter said nothing but
  'Cut us another slice:

I wish you were not quite so deaf—
    I've had to ask you twice!'

'It seems a shame,' the Walrus said,
    'To play them such a trick,
After we've brought them out so far,
    And made them trot so quick!'
The Carpenter said nothing but
    'The butter's spread too thick!'

'I weep for you,' the Walrus said:
    'I deeply sympathize.'
With sobs and tears he sorted out
    Those of the largest size,
Holding his pocket-handkerchief
    Before his streaming eyes.

'O Oysters,' said the Carpenter,
    'You've had a pleasant run!
Shall we be trotting home again?'
    But answer came there none—
And this was scarcely odd, because
    They'd eaten every one.

                              LEWIS CARROLL

A Quadrupedremian Song

He dreamt that he saw the Buffalant,
    And the spottified Dromedaraffe,
The blue Camelotamus, lean and gaunt,
    And the wild Tigeroceros calf.

The maned Liodillo loudly roared,
    And the Peccarbok whistled its whine,
The Chinchayak leapt on the dewy sward,
    As it hunted the pale Baboopine.

141

He dreamt that he met the Crocoghau,
    As it swam in the Stagnolent Lake;
But everything that in dreams he saw
    Came of eating too freely of cake.

THOMAS HOOD THE YOUNGER

[Sunset in the Sea]

... Lo! the Sun, among the daughters
    Of the sea, his chariot cools,—
Gilds the glassy-looking waters—
    Gilds the looking-glassy pools!

And the sunset sea is placid
    With its foam-line long and straight,
Fizzing like tartaric acid
    Mixed with Soda's carbonate ...

THOMAS HOOD THE YOUNGER

A Few Muddled Metaphors
By a Moore-ose Melodist

Oh, ever thus, from childhood's hour,
    I've seen my fondest hopes recede!
I never loved a tree or flow'r
    That didn't trump its partner's lead.

I never nursed a dear gazelle,
    To glad me with its dappled hide,
But, when it came to know me well.
    It fell upon the buttered side.

142

I never taught a cockatoo
  To whistle comic songs profound.
But, just when 'Jolly Dogs' it knew,
  It failed for ninepence in the pound.

I never reared a walrus-cub
  In my aquarium to plunge,
But, when it learnt to love its tub,
  It placidly threw up the sponge!

I never strove a metaphor
  To every bosom home to bring,
But—just as it had reached the door—
  It went and cut a pigeon's-wing!

THOMAS HOOD THE YOUNGER

How Singular

Though pleasures still can touch my soul,
  Though sorrow's fountain still is open—
Yet smile I not as erst I smole,
  Nor weep I as I erst have wopen.

Some years ago, in my belief,
  Life was a pudding, earth its platter;
I've pluck'd my plums of joy and grief—
  And all the rest is only batter.

THOMAS HOOD THE YOUNGER

Confounded Nonsense

Alpaca pictures of the previous past,
  Droop on the hovering confines of a snore,

And yet one further bloom, conversely vast,
  Springs bright in the perspective of the shore,

Where porphyry wings bear up an ardent pride,
  And rainbows drip from evanescent crags,
Where peaceful popinjays smile side by side,
  And immemorial franchise furls its flags.

So let it be: imperious tumbrils howl,
  And palpitating fixtures utter screeds;
Afar the murmurous aspens hoarsely scowl,
  And purple pageants echo frantic deeds.

Farewell! I see life's periphrastic orb
  Shiver to scantlings with a latent sound,
Dark ether pours, while shrinking minds absorb,
  And blatant wildernesses close around.

? THOMAS HOOD THE YOUNGER

[She lost her Sheep]

Arcuconspicilla oves looks for *perditas*,
'They'll come home, *trahentes caudas*!' What
  absurditas!

J. MOYR SMITH

[Four and Twenty Merulae]

Nummum et secalis sacculum cantate!
Four and twenty *merulae* in a pie *parate*;
Pieum when *apertum est, cecinerê crepulae*
Regi quae monstrendae, ecce pretty *epulae*!

J. MOYR SMITH

[The Fir-tree of Bosnia]

There was a young Fir-tree of Bosnia
Which daily got ros'nier and ros'nier.
   At last it caught fire
   And flamed higher and higher
And the Angels said 'My! But that was near!'

D. G. ROSSETTI

Limericks

1

There was an old man of Thermopylae,
Who never did anything properly;
But they said, 'If you choose, To boil eggs in your shoes,
You shall never remain in Thermopylae.'

2

There was an old man whose despair
Induced him to purchase a hare:
Whereon one fine day, he rode wholly away,
Which partly assuaged his despair.

3

There was an old person of Wick,
Who said, 'Tick-a-Tick, Tick-a-Tick;
Chickabee, Chickabaw,' And he said nothing more,
That laconic old person of Wick.

EDWARD LEAR

Limericks

1

There was an old person of Crowle,
Who lived in the nest of an owl;
When they screamed in the nest, he screamed
  out with the rest,
That depressing old person of Crowle.

2

There was a young lady of Corsica,
Who purchased a little brown saucy-cur;
Which she fed upon ham, and hot raspberry jam,
That expensive young lady of Corsica.

3

There was an old man of Spithead,
Who opened the window, and said,—
'Fil-jomble, fil-jumble, Fil-rumble-come-tumble!'
That doubtful old man of Spithead.

4

There was an old person of Grange,
Whose manners were scroobious and strange;
He sailed to St. Blubb, in a waterproof tub,
That aquatic old person of Grange.

EDWARD LEAR

from *Vers Nonsensiques*

1

'Cassez-vous, cassez-vous, cassez-vous,
O mer, sur vos froids gris cailloux!'
  Ainsi traduisait Laure

Au profit d'Isidore,
(Beau jeune homme, et son futur époux).

2

Un Marin naufragé (de Doncastre)
Pour prière, au milieu du désastre,
    Répétait à genoux
    Ces mots simples et doux:—
'Scintillez, scintillez, petit astre!'

3

Il existe une Espinstère à Tours,
Un peu vite, et qui porte toujours
    Un ulsteur peau-de-phoque,
    Un chapeau bilicoque,
Et des nicrebocqueurs en velours.

4

A Cologne est un mâitre d'hôtel
Hors du centre du ventre duquel
    Se projette une sorte
    De tiroir qui supporte
La moutarde, et le poivre, et le sel.

5

Il était un Gendarme, à Nanteuil,
Qui n'avait qu'une dent et qu'un œil;
    Mais cet œil solitaire
    Était plein de mystère,
Cette dent, d'importance et d'orgueil.

GEORGE DU MAURIER

A man hired by John Smith and Co.
Loudly declared he would tho
  Man that he saw
  Dumping dirt near his store.
The drivers, therefore, didn't do.

MARK TWAIN

The Dong with a Luminous Nose

When awful darkness and silence reign
Over the great Gromboolian plain,
  Through the long, long wintry nights;—
When the angry breakers roar
As they beat on the rocky shore;—
  When Storm-clouds brood on the towering heights
Of the Hills of the Chankly Bore:—
Then, through the vast and gloomy dark,
There moves what seems a fiery spark,
  A lonely spark with silvery rays
  Piercing the coal-black night,—
  A Meteor strange and bright:—
Hither and thither the vision strays,
  A single lurid light.

Slowly it wanders,—pauses,—creeps,—
Anon it sparkles,—flashes and leaps;
And ever as onward it gleaming goes
A light on the Bong-tree stems it throws.
And those who watch at that midnight hour

From Hall or Terrace, or lofty Tower,
Cry, as the wild light passes along,—
     'The Dong!—the Dong!
  The wandering Dong through the forest goes!
     The Dong! the Dong!
  The Dong with a luminous Nose!'

     Long years ago
   The Dong was happy and gay,
Till he fell in love with a Jumbly Girl
   Who came to those shores one day,
For the Jumblies came in a sieve, they did,—
Landing at eve near the Zemmery Fidd
     Where the Oblong Oysters grow,
   And the rocks are smooth and gray.
And all the woods and the valleys rang
With the Chorus they daily and nightly sang,—
        'Far and few, far and few,
        Are the lands where the Jumblies live;
        Their heads are green, and their hands are blue
        And they went to sea in a sieve.'

Happily, happily passed those days!
     While the cheerful Jumblies staid;
   They danced in circlets all night long,
   To the plaintive pipe of the lively Dong,
     In moonlight, shine, or shade.
For day and night he was always there
By the side of the Jumbly Girl so fair,
With her sky-blue hands, and her sea-green hair.
Till the morning came of that hateful day
When the Jumblies sailed in their sieve away,
And the Dong was left on the cruel shore

Gazing—gazing for evermore,—
Ever keeping his weary eyes on
That pea-green sail on the far horizon,—
Singing the Jumbly Chorus still
As he sate all day on the grassy hill,—
    'Far and few, far and few,
    Are the lands where the Jumblies live;
    Their heads are green, and their hands are blue,
    And they went to sea in a sieve.'

But when the sun was low in the West,
    The Dong arose and said;—
—'What little sense I once possessed
    Has quite gone out of my head!'—
And since that day he wanders still
By lake and forest, marsh and hill,
Singing—'O somewhere, in valley or plain
Might I find my Jumbly Girl again!
For ever I'll seek by lake and shore
Till I find my Jumbly Girl once more!'

        Playing a pipe with silvery squeaks,
        Since then his Jumbly Girl he seeks,
        And because by night he could not see,
        He gathered the bark of the Twangum Tree
            On the flowery plain that grows.
            And he wove him a wondrous Nose,—
            A Nose as strange as a Nose could be!
Of vast proportions and painted red,
And tied with cords to the back of his head.
            —In a hollow rounded space it ended
            With a luminous Lamp within suspended,
                All fenced about
                With a bandage stout

To prevent the wind from blowing it out;—
And with holes all round to send the light,
In gleaming rays on the dismal night.

And now each night, and all night long,
Over those plains still roams the Dong;
And above the wail of the Chimp and Snipe
You may hear the squeak of his plaintive pipe
While ever he seeks, but seeks in vain
To meet with his Jumbly Girl again;
Lonely and wild—all night he goes,—
The Dong with a luminous Nose!
And all who watch at the midnight hour,
From Hall or Terrace, or lofty Tower,
Cry, as they trace the Meteor bright,
Moving along through the dreary night,—
'This is the hour when forth he goes,
The Dong with a luminous Nose!
Yonder—over the plain he goes;
He goes!
He goes;
The Dong with a luminous Nose!'

EDWARD LEAR

Limericks

I

There was an Old Man of the Dee,
Who was sadly annoyed by a flea;
When he said, 'I will scratch it'—they gave him a hatchet,
Which grieved that Old Man of the Dee.

There was an old man of El Hums,
Who lived upon nothing but crumbs,
Which he picked off the ground, with the other birds round,
In the roads and the lanes of El Hums.

There was an old person of Bar,
Who passed all her life in a jar,
Which she painted pea-green, to appear more serene,
That placid old person of Bar.

There was an old man in a tree,
Whose whiskers were lovely to see;
But the birds of the air, pluck'd them perfectly bare,
To make themselves nests in that tree.

EDWARD LEAR

Menu

Potage
Potage au Petit Puss.

(*Pour Poisson*)
Queues de Chat, a l'Anguille.

Ière Entrée
Oreilles de Chat, frites à la
Kilkenny.
Pattes de Chat—aux châtaignes.

2ème Entrèe
Cotelettes de petit chat (sauce
doigts de pied de Martyr—
Tomata Sauce).

Roti
Gros Chat Noir.

Pour Légume
De Terre—sans pommes. Petit-
es Pierrès cuites à l'eau
chaude.

Gibier
Croquette aux balles.
Canards de Malta.
Sauce au poivre,
Sauce au sel.

Patisserie
Pâté de vers de soie au sucre, breadcrumbs
à l'Oliver Cromwell
(all of a crumble).
Boudin de Mille Mouches.
Compote de Mouches Noires.

EDWARD LEAR

The Courtship of the Yonghy-Bonghy-Bò

[1]
On the Coast of Coromandel
Where the early pumpkins blow,
In the middle of the woods
Lived the Yonghy-Bonghy-Bò.

Two old chairs, and half a candle,—
One old jug without a handle,—
    These were all his worldly goods:
    In the middle of the woods,
    These were all the worldly goods,
Of the Yonghy-Bonghy-Bò,
Of the Yonghy-Bonghy-Bò.

[II]

Once, among the Bong-trees walking
    Where the early pumpkins blow,
    To a little heap of stones
    Came the Yonghy-Bonghy-Bò.
There he heard a Lady talking,
To some milk-white Hens of Dorking,—
    "Tis the Lady Jingly Jones!
    On that little heap of stones
    Sits the Lady Jingly Jones!'
Said the Yonghy-Bonghy-Bò,
Said the Yonghy-Bonghy-Bò.

[III]

Lady Jingly! Lady Jingly!
    Sitting where the pumpkins blow,
    Will you come and be my wife?'
Said the Yonghy-Bonghy-Bò.
'I am tired of living singly,—
On this coast so wild and shingly,—
    I'm a-weary of my life:
    If you'll come and be my wife,
    Quite serene would be my life!'—
Said the Yonghy-Bonghy-Bò,
Said the Yonghy-Bonghy-Bò.

[IV]

'On this Coast of Coromandel,
    Shrimps and watercresses grow,

Prawns are plentiful and cheap,'
Said the Yonghy-Bonghy-Bò.
'You shall have my Chairs and candle,
And my jug without a handle!—
    Gaze upon the rolling deep
    (Fish is plentiful and cheap)
    As the sea, my love is deep!'
Said the Yonghy-Bonghy-Bò,
Said the Yonghy-Bonghy-Bò.

[v]

Lady Jingly answered sadly,
    And her tears began to flow,—
        'Your proposal comes too late,
    Mr. Yonghy-Bonghy-Bò!
I would be your wife most gladly!'
(Here she twirled her fingers madly,)
        'But in England I've a mate!
        Yes! you've asked me far too late,
        For in England I've a mate,
    Mr. Yonghy-Bonghy-Bò!
    Mr. Yonghy-Bonghy-Bò!'

[VI]

'Mr. Jones—(his name is Handel,—
    Handel Jones, Esquire, & Co.)
        Dorking fowls delights to send,
    Mr. Yonghy-Bonghy-Bò!
Keep, oh! keep your chairs and candle,
And your jug without a handle,—
        I can merely be your friend!
        —Should my Jones more Dorkings send,
        I will give you three, my friend!
    Mr. Yonghy-Bonghy-Bò!
    Mr. Yonghy-Bonghy-Bò!

'Though you've such a tiny body,
    And your head so large doth grow,—
        Though your hat may blow away,
    Mr. Yonghy-Bonghy-Bò!
Though you're such a Hoddy Doddy—
Yet I wish that I could modi-
        fy the words I needs must say!
        Will you please to go away?
        That is all I have to say—
    Mr. Yonghy-Bonghy-Bò!
    Mr. Yonghy-Bonghy-Bò!'

[VIII]

Down the slippery slopes of Myrtle,
    Where the early pumpkins blow,
        To the calm and silent sea
    Fled the Yonghy-Bonghy-Bò.
There, beyond the Bay of Gurtle,
Lay a large and lively Turtle;—
        'You're the Cove,' he said, 'for me
        On your back beyond the sea,
        Turtle, you shall carry me!'
    Said the Yonghy-Bonghy-Bò,
    Said the Yonghy-Bonghy-Bò.

[IX]

Through the silent-roaring ocean
    Did the Turtle swiftly go;
        Holding fast upon his shell
    Rode the Yonghy-Bonghy-Bò.
With a sad primæval motion
Towards the sunset isles of Boshen
        Still the Turtle bore him well.
        Holding fast upon his shell,
        'Lady Jingly Jones, farewell!'

Sang the Yonghy-Bonghy-Bò.
Sang the Yonghy-Bonghy-Bò.

[x]
From the Coast of Coromandel,
  Did that Lady never go;
    On that heap of stones she mourns
  For the Yonghy-Bonghy-Bò.
On that Coast of Coromandel,
In his jug without a handle
    Still she weeps, and daily moans;
    On that little heap of stones
    To her Dorking Hens she moans,
  For the Yonghy-Bonghy-Bò,
  For the Yonghy-Bonghy-Bò.

EDWARD LEAR

Cold are the Crabs

Cold are the crabs that crawl on yonder hills,
Colder the cucumbers that grow beneath,
And colder still the brazen chops that wreathe
  The tedious gloom of philosophic pills!
For when the tardy film of nectar fills
The ample bowls of demons and of men,
There lurks the feeble mouse, the homely hen,
  And there the porcupine with all her quills.
Yet much remains—to weave a solemn strain
That lingering sadly—slowly dies away,
Daily departing with departing day
A pea green gamut on a distant plain
When wily walrusses in congress meet—
  Such such is life—

EDWARD LEAR

Scraps of Lear

1

Saith the Poet of Nonsense
'Thoughts into my head do come
Thick as flies upon a plum.'

2

<Wet Weather at Cannes>
O pumpkins! O periwinkles!
O pobblesquattles! how him rain!

3

I feel like 5 nutmeg-graters full of baked egg shells—so cold &
dry & miserable.

4

I have no more energy than a shrimp who has swallowed a
Norfolk Dumpling.

EDWARD LEAR

After Tennyson

1

To watch the tipsy cripples on the beach,
With topsy turvy signs of screamy play.

2

Spoonmeat at Bill Porter's in the Hall,
Wit'. green pomegranates, and no end of Bass.

EDWARD LEAR

More Scraps of Lear

1

... Looking out on the sounding syllabub sea and the obvious octagonal ocean ...

2

'Een in our hashes live their wonted fires'—as the poetical cook said when they said her hashed mutton was not hot enough.

3
[His Doctor]

Hassall irritates me by his damned Thermometers and Barometers. As If I couldn't tell when an East wind cuts me in half—spite of the thermometer—by reason of sunshine—being ever so high!! I told him just now that I had ordered a baked Barometer for dinner, and 2 Thermometers stewed in treacle for supper.

EDWARD LEAR

The Pelican Chorus

King and Queen of the Pelicans we;
No other Birds so grand we see!
None but we have feet like fins!
With lovely leathery throats and chins!
 Ploffskin, Pluffskin, Pelican jee!
 We think no Birds so happy as we!
 Plumpskin, Ploshkin, Pelican jill!
 We think so then, and we thought so still!

We live on the Nile. The Nile we love.
By night we sleep on the cliffs above;
By day we fish, and at eve we stand
On long bare islands of yellow sand.
And when the sun sinks slowly down

159

And the great rock walls grow dark and brown,
Where the purple river rolls fast and dim
And the Ivory Ibis starlike skim,
Wing to wing we dance around,—
Stamping our feet with a flumpy sound,—
Opening our mouths as Pelicans ought,
And this is the song we nightly snort;—
　　Ploffskin, Pluffskin, Pelican jee,—
　　We think no Birds so happy as we!
　　Plumpskin, Ploshkin, Pelican jill,—
　　We think so then, and we thought so still.

Last year came out our Daughter, Dell;
And all the Birds received her well.
To do her honour, a feast we made
For every bird that can swim or wade.
Herons and Gulls, and Cormorants black,
Cranes, and Flamingoes with scarlet back,
Plovers and Storks, and Geese in clouds,
Swans and Dilberry Ducks in crowds.
Thousands of Birds in wondrous flight!
They ate and drank and danced all night,
And echoing back from the rocks you heard
Multitude-echoes from Bird and Bird,—
　　Ploffskin, Pluffskin, Pelican jee,
　　We think no Birds so happy as we!
　　Plumpskin, Ploshkin, Pelican jill,
　　We think so then, and we thought so still!

Yes, they came; and among the rest,
The King of the Cranes all grandly dressed.
Such a lovely tail! Its feathers float
Between the ends of his blue dress-coat;
With pea-green trowsers all so neat,
And a delicate frill to hide his feet,—
(For though no one speaks of it, every one knows,
He has got no webs between his toes!)

As soon as he saw our Daughter Dell,
In violent love that Crane King fell,—
On seeing her waddling form so fair,
With a wreath of shrimps in her short white hair.
And before the end of the next long day,
Our Dell had given her heart away;
For the King of the Cranes had won that heart,
With a Crocodile's egg and a large fish-tart.
She vowed to marry the King of the Cranes,
Leaving the Nile for stranger plains;
And away they flew in a gathering crowd
Of endless birds in a lengthening cloud.
    Ploffskin, Pluffskin, Pelican jee,
      We think no Birds so happy as we!
    Plumpskin, Ploshkin, Pelican jill,
      We think so then, and we thought so still!

And far away in the twilight sky,
We heard them singing a lessening cry,—
Farther and farther till out of sight,
And we stood alone in the silent night!
Often since, in the nights of June,
We sit on the sand and watch the moon;—
She has gone to the great Gromboolian plain,
And we probably never shall meet again!
Oft, in the long still nights of June,
We sit on the rocks and watch the moon;—
——She dwells by the streams of the Chankly Bore,
And we probably never shall see her more.
    Ploffskin, Pluffskin, Pelican jee,
      We think no Birds so happy as we!
    Plumpskin, Ploshkin, Pelican jill,
      We think so then, and we thought so still!

EDWARD LEAR

Ferdinando and Elvira;

Or, the Gentle Pieman

Part I

At a pleasant evening party I had taken down to supper
One whom I will call ELVIRA, and we talked of love and
  TUPPER.

MR. TUPPER and the Poets, very lightly with them dealing,
For I've always been distinguished for a strong poetic feeling.

Then we let off paper crackers, each of which contained a
  motto,
And she listened while I read them, till her mother told her
  not to.

Then she whispered, 'To the ball-room we had better, dear,
  be walking;
If we stop down here much longer, really people will be
  talking.'

There were noblemen in coronets, and military cousins,
There were captains by the hundred, there were baronets by
  dozens.

Yet she heeded not their offers, but dismissed them with a
  blessing,
Then she let down all her back hair, which had taken long in
  dressing.

Then she had convulsive sobbings in her agitated throttle,
Then she wiped her pretty eyes and smelt her pretty
  smelling-bottle.

So I whispered, 'Dear ELVIRA, say,—what can the matter be
    with you?
Does anything you've eaten, darling POPSY, disagree with
    you?'

But spite of all I said, her sobs grew more and more distressing,
And she tore her pretty back hair, which had taken long in
    dressing.

Then she gazed upon the carpet, at the ceiling, then above me,
And she whispered, 'FERDINANDO, do you really, *really* love
    me?'

'Love you?' said I, then I sighed, and then I gazed upon her
    sweetly—
For I think I do this sort of thing particularly neatly.

'Send me to the Arctic regions, or illimitable azure,
On a scientific goose-chase, with my COXWELL or my
    GLAISHER!

'Tell me whither I may hie me—tell me, dear one, that I may
    know—
Is it up the highest Andes? down a horrible volcano?'

But she said, 'It isn't polar bears, or hot volcanic grottoes:
Only find out who it is that writes those lovely cracker
    mottoes!'

Part II

'Tell me, HENRY WADSWORTH, ALFRED, POET CLOSE, or
    MISTER TUPPER.
Do you write the bon bon mottoes my ELVIRA pulls at supper?'

But HENRY WADSWORTH smiled, and said he had not had that
    honour;

And ALFRED, too, disclaimed the words that told so much
   upon her.

'MISTER MARTIN TUPPER, POET CLOSE, I beg of you inform us;'
But my question seemed to throw them both into a rage
   enormous.

MISTER CLOSE expressed a wish that he could only get anigh
   to me;
And MISTER MARTIN TUPPER sent the following reply to me:

'A fool is bent upon a twig, but wise men dread a bandit,'—
Which I know was very clever; but I didn't understand it.

Seven weary years I wandered—Patagonia, China, Norway,
Till at last I sank exhausted at a pastrycook his doorway.

There were fuchsias and geraniums, and daffodils and myrtle,
So I entered, and I ordered half a basin of mock turtle.

He was plump and he was chubby, he was smooth and he was
   rosy,
And his little wife was pretty and particularly cosy.

And he chirped and sang, and skipped about, and laughed with
   laughter hearty—
He was wonderfully active for so very stout a party.

And I said, 'O gentle pieman, why so very, very merry?
Is it purity of conscience, or your one-and-seven sherry?'

But he answered, 'I'm so happy—no profession could be
   dearer—
If I am not humming "Tra! la! la!" I'm singing "Tirer, lirer!"

'First I go and make the patties, and the puddings, and the
   jellies,

Then I make a sugar bird-cage, which upon a table swell is;

'Then I polish all the silver, which a supper-table lacquers;
Then I write the pretty mottoes which you find inside the
    crackers.'—

'Found at last!' I madly shouted. 'Gentle pieman, you astound
    me!'
Then I waved the turtle soup enthusiastically round me.

And I shouted and I danced until he'd quite a crowd around
    him—
And I rushed away exclaiming, 'I have found him! I have
    found him!'

And I heard the gentle pieman in the road behind me trilling,
' "Tira, lira!" stop him, stop him! "Tra! la! la!" the soup's a
    shilling!'

But until I reached ELVIRA's home, I never, never waited,
And ELVIRA to her FERDINAND's irrevocably mated!

W. S. GILBERT

To the Terrestrial Globe

by a Miserable Wretch

Roll on, thou ball, roll on!
Through pathless realms of Space
          Roll on!
What though I'm in a sorry case?
What though I cannot meet my bills?
What though I suffer toothache's ills?
What though I swallow countless pills?
          Never *you* mind!
          Roll on!

Roll on, thou ball, roll on!
Through seas of inky air
        Roll on!
It's true I've got no shirts to wear;
It's true my butcher's bill is due;
It's true my prospects all look blue—
But don't let that unsettle you!
        Never *you* mind!
        Roll on!

> [*It rolls on.*

W. S. GILBERT

The Owl and The Pussy-cat

[I]

The Owl and the Pussy-cat went to sea
    In a beautiful pea-green boat,
They took some honey, and plenty of money,
    Wrapped up in a five-pound note.
The Owl looked up to the stars above,
    And sang to a small guitar,
'O lovely Pussy! O Pussy, my love,
    What a beautiful Pussy you are,
        You are,
        You are!
What a beautiful Pussy you are!'

[II]

Pussy said to the Owl, 'You elegant fowl!
    How charmingly sweet you sing!
O let us be married! too long we have tarried:
    But what shall we do for a ring?'
They sailed away, for a year and a day,
    To the land where the Bong-tree grows

166

And there in a wood a Piggy-wig stood
  With a ring at the end of his nose,
        His nose,
        His nose,
  With a ring at the end of his nose.

[III]

'Dear Pig, are you willing to sell for one shilling
  Your ring?' Said the Piggy, 'I will.'
So they took it away, and were married next day
  By the Turkey who lives on the hill.
They dined on mince, and slices of quince,
  Which they ate with a runcible spoon;
And hand in hand, on the edge of the sand,
  They danced by the light of the moon,
        The moon,
        The moon,
  They danced by the light of the moon.

EDWARD LEAR

The Children of the Owl and the Pussy-cat *

Our mother was the Pussy-cat, our father was the Owl,
And so we're partly little beasts and partly little fowl,
The brothers of our family have feathers and they hoot,
While all the sisters dress in fur and have long tails to boot.
    We all believe that little mice,
    For food are singularly nice.
Our mother died long years ago. She was a lovely cat
Her tail was 5 feet long, and grey with stripes, but what of
    that?
In Sila forest on the East of far Calabria's shore
She tumbled from a lofty tree—none ever saw her more.
Our owly father long was ill from sorrow and surprise,

* Unfinished

167

But with the feathers of his tail he wiped his weeping eyes.
And in the hollow of a tree in Sila's inmost maze
We made a happy home and there we pass our obvious days.

From Reggian Cosenza many owls about us flit
And bring us worldly news for which we do not care a bit.
We watch the sun each morning rise, beyond Tarento's strait;
We go out ――――――― before it gets too late;
And when the evening shades begin to lengthen from the trees
――――――――― as sure as bees is bees.
We wander up and down the shore ―――――――
Or tumble over head and heels, but never, never more
Can see the far Gromboolian plains ―――――
Or weep as we could once have wept o'er many a vanished
   scene:
This is the way our father moans—he is so very green.

Our father still preserves his voice, and when he sees a star
He often sings ――――― to that original guitar.

――――――――――――――――――

――――――――――――――――

The pot in which our parents took the honey in their boat,
But all the money has been spent, beside the £5 note.
The owls who come and bring us news are often――
Because we take no interest in poltix of the day.)

EDWARD LEAR

Riddles

What saint should be the patron of Malta?
   Saint Sea-bastian.

And why are the kisses of mermaids pleasant
at breakfast?
   Because they are a kind of Water C^aresses.

When may the Lanes and Roads have shed tears
of sympathy?
When the Street'*swept.*

What letter confounds Comets and Cookery?
G—for it turns *A*stronomy into *G*astronomy.

Why are beginners on a Pianoforte like parasites
on the backs of deceased fishes?
Because they are always running up and down
their damned scales.

Why could not Eve have the measles?
Because she'd *Adam.*

EDWARD LEAR

To Make an Amblongus Pie

Take 4 pounds (say 4½ pounds) of fresh Amblongusses, and put
them in a small pipkin.

Cover them with water and boil them for 8 hours incessantly,
after which add 2 pints of new milk, and proceed to boil for 4
hours more.

When you have ascertained that the Amblongusses are quite
soft, take them out and place them in a wide pan, taking care to
shake them well previously.

Grate some nutmeg over the surface, and cover them care-
fully with powdered gingerbread, curry powder, and a sufficient
quantity of cayenne pepper.

Remove the pan into the next room, and place it on the floor.
Bring it back again, and let it simmer for three-quarters of an
hour. Shake the pan violently till all the Amblongusses have
become a pale purple colour.

Then, having prepared the paste, insert the whole carefully,
adding at the same time a small pigeon, 2 slices of beef, 4 cauli-
flowers, and any number of oysters.

Watch patiently till the crust begins to rise, and add a pinch of salt from time to time.

Serve up in a clean dish, and throw the whole out of the window as fast as possible.

EDWARD LEAR

The Jumblies

[I]

They went to sea in a Sieve, they did,
   In a Sieve they went to sea:
In spite of all their friends could say,
On a winter's morn, on a stormy day,
   In a Sieve they went to sea!
And when the Sieve turned round and round,
And every one cried, 'You'll all be drowned!'
They called aloud, 'Our Sieve ain't big,
But we don't care a button! we don't care a fig!
   In a Sieve we'll go to sea!'
      Far and few, far and few,
        Are the lands where the Jumblies live;
      Their heads are green, and their hands are blue,
        And they went to sea in a Sieve.

[II]

They sailed in a Sieve, they did,
   In a Sieve they sailed so fast,
With only a beautiful pea-green veil
Tied with a riband by way of a sail,
   To a small tobacco-pipe mast;
And every one said, who saw them go,
'O won't they be soon upset, you know!
For the sky is dark, and the voyage is long,
And happen what may, it's extremely wrong

In a Sieve to sail so fast!'
   Far and few, far and few,
      Are the lands where the Jumblies live;
   Their heads are green, and their hands are blue,
      And they went to sea in a Sieve.

[III]

The water it soon came in, it did,
   The water it soon came in;
So to keep them dry, they wrapped their feet
In a pinky paper all folded neat,
   And they fastened it down with a pin.
And they passed the night in a crockery-jar,
And each of them said, 'How wise we are!
Though the sky be dark, and the voyage be long,
Yet we never can think we were rash or wrong,
   While round in our Sieve we spin!'
   Far and few, far and few,
      Are the lands where the Jumblies live;
   Their heads are green, and their hands are blue,
      And they went to sea in a Sieve.

[IV]

And all night long they sailed away;
   And when the sun went down,
They whistled and warbled a moony song
To the echoing sound of a coppery gong,
   In the shade of the mountains brown.
'O Timballo! How happy we are,
When we live in a sieve and a crockery-jar,
And all night long in the moonlight pale,
We sail away with a pea-green sail,
   In the shade of the mountains brown!'
   Far and few, far and few,
      Are the lands where the Jumblies live;
   Their heads are green, and their hands are blue,
      And they went to sea in a Sieve.

[V]

They sailed to the Western Sea, they did,
   To a land all covered with trees,
And they bought an Owl, and a useful Cart,
And a pound of Rice, and a Cranberry Tart,
   And a hive of silvery Bees.
And they bought a Pig, and some green Jack-daws,
And a lovely Monkey with lollipop paws,
And forty bottles of Ring-Bo-Ree,
   And no end of Stilton Cheese.
     Far and few, far and few,
      Are the lands where the Jumblies live;
     Their heads are green, and their hands are blue,
      And they went to sea in a Sieve.

[VI]

And in twenty years they all came back,
   In twenty years or more,
And every one said, 'How tall they've grown!
For they've been to the Lakes, and the Torrible Zone,
   And the hills of the Chankly Bore;
And they drank their health, and gave them a feast
Of dumplings made of beautiful yeast;
And every one said, 'If we only live,
We too will go to sea in a Sieve,—
   To the hills of the Chankly Bore!'
     Far and few, far and few,
      Are the lands where the Jumblies live;
     Their heads are green, and their hands are blue,
      And they went to sea in a Sieve.

EDWARD LEAR

[Mrs. Jaypher]

Mrs. Jaypher found a wafer
Which she stuck upon a note;
This she took and gave the cook.
Then she went and bought a boat
Which she paddled down the stream
Shouting, 'Ice produces cream,
Beer when churned produces butter!
Henceforth all the words I utter
Distant ages thus shall note—
"From the Jaypher Wisdom-Boat." '

EDWARD LEAR

[Mrs. Jaypher on Lemons]

Mrs. Jaypher said it's safer
If you've lemons in your head
First to eat a pound of meat
And then to go at once to bed.

EDWARD LEAR

Dingle Bank

He lived at Dingle Bank—he did;—
    He lived at Dingle Bank;
And in his garden was one Quail,
    Four tulips, and a Tank:
And from his windows he could see
The otion and the River Dee.

173

His house stood on a Cliff,—it did,
　Its aspic it was cool;
And many thousand little boys
　Resorted to his school,
Where if of progress they could boast
He gave them heaps of buttered toast.

But he grew rabid-wroth, he did,
　If they neglected books,
And dragged them to adjacent cliffs
　With beastly Button Hooks,
And there with fatuous glee he threw
Them down into the otion blue

And in the sea they swam, they did,—
　All playfully about,
And some eventually became
　Sponges or speckled trout:—
But Liverpool doth all bewail
Their Fate; likewise his Garden Quail.

EDWARD LEAR

The Chancellor's Nightmare

Love, unrequited, robs me of my rest:
　Love, hopeless love, my ardent soul encumbers:
Love, nightmare-like, lies heavy on my chest:
　And weaves itself into my midnight slumbers!

When you're lying awake with a dismal headache, and repose is
　taboo'd by anxiety,
I conceive you may use any language you choose to indulge in,
　without impropriety;
For your brain is on fire—the bedclothes conspire of usual slum-
　ber to plunder you:

174

First your counterpane goes, and uncovers your toes, and your
    sheets slips demurely from under you;
Then the blanketing tickles—you feel like mixed pickles—so
    terribly sharp is the pricking.
And you're hot, and you're cross, and you tumble and toss till
    there's nothing 'twixt you and the ticking.
Then the bedclothes all creep to the ground in a heap, and you
    pick 'em all up in a tangle;
Next your pillow resigns and politely declines to remain at its
    usual angle!
Well, you get some repose in the form of a doze, with hot eye-
    balls and head ever aching,
But your slumbering teems with such horrible dreams that you'd
    very much better be waking;
For you dream you are crossing the Channel, and tossing about
    in a steamer from Harwich—
Which is something between a large bathing machine and a very
    small second-class carriage—
And you're giving a treat (penny ice and cold meat) to a party of
    friends and relations—
They're a ravenous horde—and they all came on board at Sloane
    Square and South Kensington Stations.
And bound on that journey you find your attorney (who started
    that morning from Devon);
He's a bit undersized, and you don't feel surprised when he tells
    you he's only eleven.
Well, you're driving like mad with this singular lad (by the by,
    the ship's now a four-wheeler),
And you're playing round games, and he calls you bad names
    when you tell him that 'ties pay the dealer';
But this you can't stand, so you throw up your hand, and you
    find you're as cold as an icicle,
In your shirt and your socks (the black silk with gold clocks),
    crossing Salisbury Plain on a bicycle:
And he and the crew are on bicycles too—which they've some-
    how or other invested in—

And he's telling the tars all the particu*lars* of a company he's
   interested in—
It's a scheme of devices, to get at low prices all goods from cough
   mixtures to cables
(Which tickled the sailors,) by treating retailers as though they
   were all vege*t*ables—
You get a good spadesman to plant a small tradesman (first take
   off his boots with a boot-tree),
And his legs will take root, and his fingers will shoot, and they'll
   blossom and bud like a fruit-tree—
From the greengrocer tree you get grapes and green pea, cauli-
   flower, pineapple, and cranberries,
While the pastrycook plant cherry brandy will grant, apple
   puffs, and three-corners, and Banburys—
The shares are a penny, and ever so many are taken by Rothschild
   and Baring,
And just as a few are allotted to you, you awake with a shudder
   despairing—
You're a regular wreck, with a crick in your neck, and no wonder
   you snore, for your head's on the floor, and you've needles and
   pins from your soles to your shins, and your flesh is a-creep, for
   your left leg's asleep, and you've cramp in your toes, and a fly
   on your nose, and a thirst that's intense, and a general sense that
   you haven't been sleeping in clover;
But the darkness has passed, and it's daylight at last, and the night
   has been long—ditto ditto my song—and thank goodness
   they're both of them over!

W. S. GILBERT

Oh, Hollow! Hollow! Hollow!

What time the poet hath hymned
The writhing maid, lithe-limbed,
   Quivering on amaranthine asphodel,
How can he paint her woes,

Knowing, as well he knows,
   That all can be set right with calomel?

When from the poet's plinth
The amorous colocynth
   Yearns for the aloe, faint with rapturous thrills,
How can he hymn their throes,
Knowing, as well he knows,
   That they are only uncompounded pills?

Is it, and can it be,
Nature hath this decree,
   Nothing poetic in the world shall dwell?
Or that in all her works
Something poetic lurks,
   Even in colocynth and calomel?
      I cannot tell.

W. S. GILBERT

The Hunting of the Snark

An Agony in Eight Fits

Fit the First

THE LANDING

'Just the place for a Snark!' the Bellman cried,
   As he landed his crew with care;
Supporting each man on the top of the tide
   By a finger entwined in his hair.

'Just the place for a Snark! I have said it twice:
   That alone should encourage the crew.
Just the place for a Snark! I have said it thrice:
   What I tell you three times is true.'

The crew was complete: it included a Boots—
   A maker of Bonnets and Hoods—
A Barrister, brought to arrange their disputes—
   And a Broker, to value their goods.

A Billiard-marker, whose skill was immense,
   Might perhaps have won more than his share—
But a Banker, engaged at enormous expense,
   Had the whole of their cash in his care.

There was also a Beaver, that paced on the deck,
   Or would sit making lace in the bow:
And had often (the Bellman said) saved them from wreck,
   Though none of the sailors knew how.

There was one who was famed for the number of things
   He forgot when he entered the ship:
His umbrella, his watch, all his jewels and rings,
   And the clothes he had bought for the trip.

He had forty-two boxes, all carefully packed,
   With his name painted clearly on each:
But, since he omitted to mention the fact,
   They were all left behind on the beach.

The loss of his clothes hardly mattered, because
   He had seven coats on when he came,
With three pair of boots——but the worst of it was,
   He had wholly forgotten his name.

He would answer to 'Hi!' or to any loud cry,
   Such as 'Fry me!' or 'Fritter my wig!'
To 'What-you-may-call-um!' or 'What-was-his-name!'
   But especially 'Thing-um-a-jig!'

While, for those who preferred a more forcible word,
   He had different names from these:
His intimate friends called him 'Candle-ends,'
   And his enemies 'Toasted-cheese.'

'His form is ungainly——his intellect small——'
   (So the Bellman would often remark)
'But his courage is perfect! And that, after all,
   Is the thing that one needs with a Snark.'

He would joke with hyænas, returning their stare
   With an impudent wag of the head:
And he once went a walk, paw-in-paw, with a bear,
   'Just to keep up its spirits,' he said.

He came as a Baker: but owned when too late—
   And it drove the poor Bellman half-mad—
He could only bake Bridecake——for which, I may state,
   No materials were to be had.

The last of the crew needs especial remark,
   Though he looked an incredible dunce:
He had just one idea——but, that one being 'Snark,'
   The good Bellman engaged him at once.

He came as a Butcher: but gravely declared,
   When the ship had been sailing a week,
He could only kill Beavers. The Bellman looked scared,
   And was almost too frightened to speak:

But at length he explained, in a tremulous tone,
   There was only one Beaver on board;
And that was a tame one he had of his own,
   Whose death would be deeply deplored.

The Beaver, who happened to hear the remark,
  Protested, with tears in its eyes,
That not even the rapture of hunting the Snark
  Could atone for that dismal surprise!

It strongly advised that the Butcher should be
  Conveyed in a separate ship:
But the Bellman declared that would never agree
  With the plans he had made for the trip:

Navigation was always a difficult art,
  Though with only one ship and one bell:
And he feared he must really decline, for his part,
  Undertaking another as well.

The Beaver's best course was, no doubt, to procure
  A second-hand dagger-proof coat——
So the Baker advised it——and next, to insure
  Its life in some Office of note:

This the Baker suggested, and offered for hire
  (On moderate terms), or for sale,
Two excellent Policies, one Against Fire,
  And one Against Damage From Hail.

Yet still, ever after that sorrowful day,
  Whenever the Butcher was by,
The Beaver kept looking the opposite way,
  And appeared unaccountably shy.

Fit the Second
THE BELLMAN'S SPEECH

The Bellman himself they all praised to the skies——
  Such a carriage, such ease and such grace!
Such solemnity, too! One could see he was wise,
  The moment one looked in his face!

He had bought a large map representing the sea,
  Without the least vestige of land:
And the crew were much pleased when they found it to be
  A map they could all understand.

'What's the good of Mercator's North Poles and Equators,
  Tropics, Zones, and Meridian Lines?'
So the Bellman would cry: and the crew would reply,
  'They are merely conventional signs!

'Other maps are such shapes, with their islands and capes!
  But we've got our brave Captain to thank'
(So the crew would protest) 'that he's bought us the best——
  A perfect and absolute blank!'

This was charming, no doubt: but they shortly found out
  That the Captain they trusted so well
Had only one notion for crossing the ocean,
  And that was to tingle his bell.

He was thoughtful and grave——but the orders he gave
  Were enough to bewilder a crew.
When he cried, 'Steer to starboard, but keep her head
    larboard!'
  What on earth was the helmsman to do?

Then the bowsprit got mixed with the rudder sometimes:
  A thing, as the Bellman remarked,
That frequently happens in tropical climes,
  When a vessel is, so to speak, 'snarked.'

But the principal failing occurred in the sailing,
  And the Bellman, perplexed and distressed,
Said he *had* hoped, at least, when the wind blew due East
  That the ship would *not* travel due West!

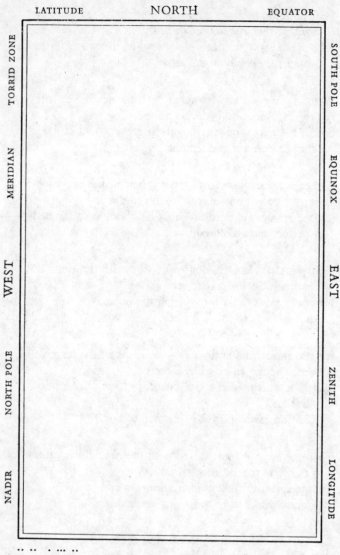

LATITUDE   NORTH   EQUATOR

TORRID ZONE

MERIDIAN

WEST

NORTH POLE

NADIR

SOUTH POLE

EQUINOX

EAST

ZENITH

LONGITUDE

Scale of Miles

OCEAN-CHART

But the danger was past——they had landed at last,
  With their boxes, portmanteaus, and bags:
Yet at first sight the crew were not pleased with the view,
  Which consisted of chasms and crags.

The Bellman perceived that their spirits were low,
  And repeated in musical tone
Some jokes he had kept for a season of woe——
  But the crew would do nothing but groan.

He served out some grog with a liberal hand,
  And bade them sit down on the beach:
And they could not but own that their Captain looked grand,
  As he stood and delivered his speech.

'Friends, Romans, and countrymen, lend me your ears!'
  (They were all of them fond of quotations:
So they drank to his health, and they gave him three cheers,
  While he served out additional rations.)

'We have sailed many months, we have sailed many weeks
  (Four weeks to the month you may mark),
But never as yet ('tis your Captain who speaks)
  Have we caught the least glimpse of a Snark!

'We have sailed many weeks, we have sailed many days
  (Seven days to the week I allow),
But a Snark, on the which we might lovingly gaze,
  We have never beheld till now!

'Come, listen, my men, while I tell you again
  The five unmistakable marks
By which you may know, wheresoever you go,
  The warranted genuine Snarks.

'Let us take them in order. The first is the taste,
  Which is meagre and hollow, but crisp:

Like a coat that is rather too tight in the waist,
    With a flavour of Will-o'-the-wisp.

'Its habit of getting up late you'll agree
    That it carries too far, when I say
That it frequently breakfasts at five-o'clock tea,
    And dines on the following day.

'The third is its slowness in taking a jest,
    Should you happen to venture on one,
It will sigh like a thing that is deeply distressed:
    And it always looks grave at a pun.

'The fourth is its fondness for bathing-machines,
    Which it constantly carries about,
And believes that they add to the beauty of scenes——
    A sentiment open to doubt.

'The fifth is ambition. It next will be right
    To describe each particular batch:
Distinguishing those that have feathers, and bite,
    From those that have whiskers, and scratch.

'For, although common Snarks do no manner of harm,
    Yet, I feel it my duty to say,
Some are Boojums——' The Bellman broke off in alarm,
    For the Baker had fainted away.

Fit the Third

THE BAKER'S TALE

They roused him with muffins—they roused him with ice—
    They roused him with mustard and cress—
They roused him with jam and judicious advice—
    They set him conundrums to guess.

When at length he sat up and was able to speak,
  His sad story he offered to tell;
And the Bellman cried 'Silence! not even a shriek!'
  And excitedly tingled his bell.

There was silence supreme! Not a shriek, not a scream,
  Scarcely even a howl or a groan,
As the man they called 'Ho!' told his story of woe
  In an antediluvian tone.

'My father and mother were honest, though poor——'
  'Skip all that!' cried the Bellman in haste.
'If it once becomes dark, there's no chance of a Snark——
  We have hardly a minute to waste!'

'I skip forty years,' said the Baker, in tears,
  'And proceed without further remark
To the day when you took me aboard of your ship
  To help you in hunting the Snark.

'A dear uncle of mine (after whom I was named)
  Remarked, when I bade him farewell——'
'Oh, skip your dear uncle!' the Bellman exclaimed,
  As he angrily tingled his bell.

'He remarked to me then,' said that mildest of men,
  ' "If your Snark be a Snark, that is right:
Fetch it home by all means——you may serve it with greens,
  And it's handy for striking a light.

' "You may seek it with thimbles—and seek it with care;
  You may hunt it with forks and hope;
You may threaten its life with a railway-share;
  You may charm it with smiles and soap—" '

('That's exactly the method,' the Bellman bold
  In a hasty parenthesis cried,

185

'That's exactly the way I have always been told
    That the capture of Snarks should be tried!')

' "But oh, beamish nephew, beware of the day,
    If your Snark be a Boojum! For then
You will softly and suddenly vanish away,
    And never be met with again!"

'It is this, it is this that oppresses my soul,
    When I think of my uncle's last words:
And my heart is like nothing so much as a bowl
    Brimming over with quivering curds!

'It is this, it is this——' 'We have had that before!'
    The Bellman indignantly said.
And the Baker replied, 'Let me say it once more.
    It is this, it is this that I dread!

'I engage with the Snark——every night after dark——
    In a dreamy delirious fight:
I serve it with greens in those shadowy scenes,
    And I use it for striking a light;

'But if ever I meet with a Boojum, that day,
    In a moment (of this I am sure),
I shall softly and suddenly vanish away—
    And the notion I cannot endure!'

Fit the Fourth

THE HUNTING

The Bellman looked uffish, and wrinkled his brow.
    'If only you'd spoken before!
It's excessively awkward to mention it now,
    With the Snark, so to speak, at the door!

'We should all of us grieve, as you well may believe,
    If you never were met with again——
But surely, my man, when the voyage began,
    You might have suggested it then?

'It's excessively awkward to mention it now—
    As I think I've already remarked.'
And the man they called 'Hi!' replied, with a sigh,
    'I informed you the day we embarked.

'You may charge me with murder—or want of sense—
    (We are all of us weak at times):
But the slightest approach to a false pretence
    Was never among my crimes!

'I said it in Hebrew—I said it in Dutch—
    I said it in German and Greek;
But I wholly forgot (and it vexes me much)
    That English is what you speak!'

' 'Tis a pitiful tale,' said the Bellman, whose face
    Had grown longer at every word;
'But, now that you've stated the whole of your case,
    More debate would be simply absurd.

'The rest of my speech' (he explained to his men)
    'You shall hear when I've leisure to speak it.
But the Snark is at hand, let me tell you again!
    'Tis your glorious duty to seek it!

'To seek it with thimbles, to seek it with care;
    To pursue it with forks and hope;
To threaten its life with a railway-share;
    To charm it with smiles and soap!

'For the Snark's a peculiar creature, that won't
    Be caught in a commonplace way.

Do all that you know, and try all that you don't:
    Not a chance must be wasted to-day!

'For England expects——I forbear to proceed:
    'Tis a maxim tremendous, but trite:
And you'd best be unpacking the things that you need
    To rig yourselves out for the fight.'

Then the Banker endorsed a blank cheque (which he crossed),
    And changed his loose silver for notes.
The Baker with care combed his whiskers and hair,
    And shook the dust out of his coats.

The Boots and the Broker were sharpening a spade—
    Each working the grindstone in turn;
But the Beaver went on making lace, and displayed
    No interest in the concern:

Though the Barrister tried to appeal to its pride,
    And vainly proceeded to cite
A number of cases, in which making laces
    Had been proved an infringement of right.

The maker, of Bonnets ferociously planned
    A novel arrangement of bows:
While the Billiard-marker with quivering hand
    Was chalking the tip of his nose.

But the Butcher turned nervous, and dressed himself fine,
    With yellow kid gloves and a ruff——
Said he felt it exactly like going to dine,
    Which the Bellman declared was all 'stuff.'

'Introduce me, now there's a good fellow,' he said,
    'If we happen to meet it together!'
And the Bellman, sagaciously nodding his head,
    Said, 'That must depend on the weather.'

The Beaver went simply galumphing about,
    At seeing the Butcher so shy:
And even the Baker, though stupid and stout,
    Made an effort to wink with one eye.

'Be a man!' said the Bellman in wrath, as he heard
    The Butcher beginning to sob.
'Should we meet with a Jubjub, that desperate bird,
    We shall need all our strength for the job!'

Fit the Fifth

THE BEAVER'S LESSON

They sought it with thimbles, they sought it with care;
    They pursued it with forks and hope;
They threatened its life with a railway-share;
    They charmed it with smiles and soap.

Then the Butcher contrived an ingenious plan
    For making a separate sally;
And had fixed on a spot unfrequented by man,
    A dismal and desolate valley.

But the very same plan to the Beaver occurred:
    It had chosen the very same place;
Yet neither betrayed, by a sign or a word,
    The disgust that appeared in his face.

Each thought he was thinking of nothing but 'Snark'
    And the glorious work of the day;
And each tried to pretend that he did not remark
    That the other was going that way.

But the valley grew narrow and narrower still,
    And the evening got darker and colder,
Till (merely from nervousness, not from goodwill)
    They marched along shoulder to shoulder.

Then a scream, shrill and high, rent the shuddering sky,
  And they knew that some danger was near:
The Beaver turned pale to the tip of its tail,
  And even the Butcher felt queer.

He thought of his childhood, left far far behind—
  That blissful and innocent state—
The sound so exactly recalled to his mind
  A pencil that squeaks on a slate!

' 'Tis the voice of the Jubjub!' he suddenly cried.
  (This man, that they used to call 'Dunce.')
'As the Bellman would tell you,' he added with pride,
  'I have uttered that sentiment once.

' 'Tis the note of the Jubjub! Keep count, I entreat;
  You will find I have told it you twice.
'Tis the song of the Jubjub! The proof is complete,
  If only I've stated it thrice.'

The Beaver had counted with scrupulous care,
  Attending to every word:
But it fairly lost heart, and outgrabe in despair,
  When the third repetition occurred.

It felt that, in spite of all possible pains,
  It had somehow contrived to lose count,
And the only thing now was to rack its poor brains
  By reckoning up the amount.

'Two added to one—if that could but be done,'
  It said, 'with one's fingers and thumbs!'
Recollecting with tears how, in earlier years,
  It had taken no pains with its sums.

'The thing can be done,' said the Butcher, 'I think.
  The thing must be done, I am sure.

The thing shall be done! Bring me paper and ink,
 The best there is time to procure.'

The Beaver brought paper, portfolio, pens,
 And ink in unfailing supplies:
While strange creepy creatures came out of their dens,
 And watched them with wondering eyes.

So engrossed was the Butcher, he heeded them not,
 As he wrote with a pen in each hand,
And explained all the while in a popular style
 Which the Beaver could well understand.

'Taking Three as the subject to reason about——
 A convenient number to state——
We add Seven, and Ten, and then multiply out
 By One Thousand diminished by Eight.

'The result we proceed to divide, as you see,
 By Nine Hundred and Ninety and Two:
Then subtract Seventeen, and the answer must be
 Exactly and perfectly true.

'The method employed I would gladly explain,
 While I have it so clear in my head,
If I had but the time and you had but the brain——
 But much yet remains to be said.

'In one moment I've seen what has hitherto been
 Enveloped in absolute mystery,
And without extra charge I will give you at large
 A Lesson in Natural History.'

In his genial way he proceeded to say
 (Forgetting all laws of propriety,
And that giving instruction, without introduction,
 Would have caused quite a thrill in Society),

'As to temper the Jubjub's a desperate bird,
  Since it lives in perpetual passion:
Its taste in costume is entirely absurd——
  It is ages ahead of the fashion:

'But it knows any friend it has met once before:
  It never will look at a bribe:
And in charity-meetings it stands at the door,
  And collects——though it does not subscribe.

'Its flavour when cooked is more exquisite far
  Than mutton, or oysters, or eggs:
(Some think it keeps best in an ivory jar,
  And some, in mahogany kegs:)

'You boil it in sawdust: you salt it in glue:
  You condense it with locusts and tape:
Still keeping one principal object in view——
  To preserve its symmetrical shape.'

The Butcher would gladly have talked till next day,
  But he felt that the Lesson must end,
And he wept with delight in attempting to say
  He considered the Beaver his friend.

While the Beaver confessed, with affectionate looks
  More eloquent even than tears,
It had learnt in ten minutes far more than all books
  Would have taught it in seventy years.

They returned hand-in-hand, and the Bellman, unmanned
  (For a moment) with noble emotion,
Said, 'This amply repays all the wearisome days
  We have spent on the billowy ocean!'

Such friends, as the Beaver, and Butcher became,
  Have seldom if ever been known;

In winter or summer, 'twas always the same——
   You could never meet either alone.

And when quarrels arose——as one frequently finds
   Quarrels will, spite of every endeavour——
The song of the Jubjub recurred to their minds,
   And cemented their friendship for ever!

Fit the Sixth

THE BARRISTER'S DREAM

They sought it with thimbles, they sought it with care;
   They pursued it with forks and hope;
They threatened its life with a railway-share;
   They charmed it with smiles and soap.

But the Barrister, weary of proving in vain
   That the Beaver's lace-making was wrong,
Fell asleep, and in dreams saw the creature quite plain
   That his fancy had dwelt on so long.

He dreamed that he stood in a shadowy Court,
   Where the Snark, with a glass in its eye,
Dressed in gown, bands, and wig, was defending a pig
   On the charge of deserting its sty.

The Witnesses proved, without error or flaw,
   That the sty was deserted when found:
And the Judge kept explaining the state of the law
   In a soft under-current of sound.

The indictment had never been clearly expressed,
   And it seemed that the Snark had begun,
And had spoken three hours, before any one guessed
   What the pig was supposed to have done.

The Jury had each formed a different view
   (Long before the indictment was read),
And they all spoke at once, so that none of them knew
   One word that the others had said.

'You must know——' said the Judge: but the Snark
   exclaimed, 'Fudge!
   That statute is obsolete quite!
Let me tell you, my friends, the whole question depends
   On an ancient manorial right.

'In the matter of Treason the pig would appear
   To have aided, but scarcely abetted:
While the charge of Insolvency fails, it is clear,
   If you grant the plea "never indebted."

'The fact of Desertion I will not dispute:
   But its guilt, as I trust, is removed
(So far as relates to the costs of this suit)
   By the Alibi which has been proved.

'My poor client's fate now depends on your votes.'
   Here the speaker sat down in his place,
And directed the Judge to refer to his notes
   And briefly to sum up the case.

But the Judge said he never had summed up before;
   So the Snark undertook it instead,
And summed it so well that it came to far more
   Than the Witnesses ever had said!

When the verdict was called for, the Jury declined,
   As the word was so puzzling to spell;
But they ventured to hope that the Snark wouldn't mind
   Undertaking that duty as well.

So the Snark found the verdict, although, as it owned,
  It was spent with the toils of the day:
When it said the word 'GUILTY!' the Jury all groaned,
  And some of them fainted away.

Then the Snark pronounced sentence, the Judge being quite
  Too nervous to utter a word:
When it rose to its feet, there was silence like night,
  And the fall of a pin might be heard.

'Transportation for life' was the sentence it gave,
  'And *then* to be fined forty pound.'
The Jury all cheered, though the Judge said he feared
  That the phrase was not legally sound.

But their wild exultation was suddenly checked
  When the jailer informed them, with tears,
Such a sentence would have not the slightest effect,
  As the pig had been dead for some years.

The Judge left the Court, looking deeply disgusted:
  But the Snark, though a little aghast,
As the lawyer to whom the defence was intrusted,
  Went bellowing on to the last.

Thus the Barrister dreamed, while the bellowing seemed
  To grow every moment more clear:
Till he woke to the knell of a furious bell,
  Which the Bellman rang close at his ear.

Fit the Seventh
THE BANKER'S FATE

They sought it with thimbles, they sought it with care;
  They pursued it with forks and hope;

They threatened its life with a railway-share;
　　They charmed it with smiles and soap.

And the Banker, inspired with a courage so new
　　It was matter for general remark,
Rushed madly ahead and was lost to their view
　　In his zeal to discover the Snark.

But while he was seeking with thimbles and care,
　　A Bandersnatch swiftly drew nigh
And grabbed at the Banker, who shrieked in despair,
　　For he knew it was useless to fly.

He offered large discount—he offered a cheque
　　(Drawn 'to bearer') for seven-pounds-ten:
But the Bandersnatch merely extended its neck
　　And grabbed at the Banker again.

Without rest or pause—while those frumious jaws
　　Went savagely snapping around—
He skipped and he hopped, and he floundered and flopped,
　　Till fainting he fell to the ground.

The Bandersnatch fled as the others appeared:
　　Led on by that fear-stricken yell:
And the Bellman remarked, 'It is just as I feared!'
　　And solemnly tolled on his bell.

He was black in the face, and they scarcely could trace
　　The least likeness to what he had been:
While so great was his fright that his waistcoat turned white—
　　A wonderful thing to be seen!

To the horror of all who were present that day,
　　He uprose in full evening dress,
And with senseless grimaces endeavoured to say
　　What his tongue could no longer express.

Down he sank in a chair—ran his hands through his hair—
  And chanted in mimsiest tones
Words whose utter inanity proved his insanity,
  While he rattled a couple of bones.

'Leave him here to his fate—it is getting so late!'
  The Bellman exclaimed in a fright.
'We have lost half the day. Any further delay,
  And we shan't catch a Snark before night!'

Fit the Eighth

THE VANISHING

They sought it with thimbles, they sought it with care;
  They pursued it with forks and hope;
They threatened its life with a railway-share;
  They charmed it with smiles and soap.

They shuddered to think that the chase might fail,
  And the Beaver, excited at last,
Went bounding along on the tip of its tail,
  For the daylight was nearly past.

'There is Thingumbob shouting!' the Bellman said.
  'He is shouting like mad, only hark!
He is waving his hands, he is wagging his head,
  He has certainly found a Snark!'

They gazed in delight, while the Butcher exclaimed,
  'He was always a desperate wag!'
They beheld him—their Baker—their hero unnamed—
  On the top of a neighbouring crag,

Erect and sublime, for one moment of time.
  In the next, that wild figure they saw
(As if stung by a spasm) plunge into a chasm,
  While they waited and listened in awe.

'It's a Snark!' was the sound that first came to their ears,
  And seemed almost too good to be true.
Then followed a torrent of laughter and cheers:
  Then the ominous words, 'It's a Boo—'

Then, silence. Some fancied they heard in the air
  A weary and wandering sigh
That sounded like '—jum!' but the others declare
  It was only a breeze that went by.

They hunted till darkness came on, but they found
  Not a button, or feather, or mark,
By which they could tell that they stood on the ground
  Where the Baker had met with the Snark.

In the midst of the word he was trying to say,
  In the midst of his laughter and glee,
He had softly and suddenly vanished away——
  For the Snark *was* a Boojum, you see.

LEWIS CARROLL

More Limericks

1

There was an old person of Harrow
Who bought a mahagony barrow,
For he said to his wife, 'You're the joy of my life!
  And I'll wheel you all day in this barrow!'

2

There was an old person of Twickenham,
Who whipped his four horses to quicken 'em;
When they stood on one leg, He said faintly, 'I beg
  We may go back directly to Twickenham.'

3

There was an old man of Girgenti,
Who lived in profusion and plenty;
He lay on two chairs, And ate thousands of pears,
    That susceptible man of Girgenti.

4

There was an old man with a ribbon,
Who found a large volume of Gibbon,
Which he tied to his nose, And said, 'I suppose
    This is quite the best use for my ribbon.'

5

There was an old person of Brussels,
Who lived upon Brandy and Mussels.
When he rushed through the town, He knocked most people
    down,
    Which distressed all the people of Brussels.

EDWARD LEAR

The Pobble who has no Toes

[I]

The Pobble who has no toes
  Had once as many as we;
When they said, 'Some day you may lose them all;'—
  He replied,—'Fish fiddle de-dee!'
And his Aunt Jobiska made him drink,
Lavender water tinged with pink,
For she said, 'The World in general knows
There's nothing so good for a Pobble's toes!'

[II]

The Pobble who has no toes,
  Swam across the Bristol Channel;

But before he set out he wrapped his nose,
  In a piece of scarlet flannel.
For his Aunt Jobiska said, 'No harm
Can come to his toes if his nose is warm;
And it's perfectly known that a Pobble's toes
Are safe,—provided he minds his nose.'

[III]

The Pobble swam fast and well
  And when boats or ships came near him
He tinkledy-binkledy-winkled a bell
  So that all the world could hear him.
And all the Sailors and Admirals cried,
When they saw him nearing the further side,—
'He has gone to fish, for his Aunt Jobiska's
Runcible Cat with crimson whiskers!'

[IV]

But before he touched the shore,
  The shore of the Bristol Channel,
A sea-green Porpoise carried away
  His wrapper of scarlet flannel.
And when he came to observe his feet
Formerly garnished with toes so neat
His face at once became forlorn
On perceiving that all his toes were gone!

[V]

And nobody ever knew
  From that dark day to the present,
Whoso had taken the Pobble's toes,
  In a manner so far from pleasant.
Whether the shrimps or crawfish gray,
Or crafty Mermaids stole them away—
Nobody knew; and nobody knows
How the Pobble was robbed of his twice five toes!

The Pobble who has no toes
    Was placed in a friendly Bark,
And they rowed him back, and carried him up,
    To his Aunt Jobiska's Park.
And she made him a feast at his earnest wish
Of eggs and buttercups fried with fish;—
And she said,—'It's a fact the whole world knows,
That Pobbles are happier without their toes.'

EDWARD LEAR

Alphabet

A   tumbled down, and hurt his Arm, against a bit of wood.

B   said, 'My Boy, O! do not cry; it cannot do you good!'

C   said, 'A Cup of Coffee hot can't do you any harm.'

D   said, 'A Doctor should be fetched, and he would cure
the arm.'

E   said, 'An Egg beat up with milk would quickly make
him well.'

F   said, 'A Fish, if broiled, might cure, if only by the smell.'

G   said, 'Green Gooseberry fool, the best of cures I hold.'

H   said, 'His Hat should be kept on, to keep him from the
cold.'

I   said, 'Some Ice upon his head will make him better soon.'

J   said, 'Some Jam, if spread on bread, or given in a spoon!'

K   said, 'A Kangaroo is here,—this picture let him see.'

L   said, 'A Lamp pray keep alight, to make some barley tea.'

M said, 'A Mulberry or two might give him satisfaction.'

N said, 'Some Nuts, if rolled about, might be a slight attraction.'

O said, 'An Owl might make him laugh, if only it would wink.'

P said, 'Some Poetry might be read aloud, to make him think.'

Q said, 'A Quince I recommend,—a Quince, or else a Quail.'

R said, 'Some Rats might make him move, if fastened by their tail.'

S said, 'A Song should now be sung, in hopes to make him laugh!'

T said, 'A Turnip might avail, if sliced or cut in half!'

U said, 'An Urn, with water hot, place underneath his chin!'

V said, 'I'll stand upon a chair, and play a Violin!'

W said, 'Some Whisky-Whizzgigs fetch, some marbles and a ball!'

X said, 'Some double XX ale would be the best of all!'

Y said, 'Some Yeast mixed up with salt would make a perfect plaster!'

Z said, 'Here is a box of Zinc! Get in, my little master!
We'll shut you up! We'll nail you down!
We will, my little master!
We think we've all heard quite enough of this your sad disaster!'

EDWARD LEAR

Incidents in the Life of my
Uncle Arley

[I]

O my agèd Uncle Arly!
Sitting on a heap of Barley
    Thro' the silent hours of night,—
Close beside a leafy thicket:—
On his nose there was a Cricket,—
In his hat a Railway-Ticket;—
    (But his shoes were far too tight.)

[II]

Long ago, in youth, he squander'd
All his goods away, and wander'd
    To the Tiniskoop-hills afar.
There on golden sunsets blazing,
Every evening found him gazing,—
Singing,—'Orb! you're quite amazing!
    How I wonder what you are!'

[III]

Like the ancient Medes and Persians,
Always by his own exertions
    He subsisted on those hills;—
Whiles,—by teaching children spelling,—
Or at times by merely yelling,—
Or at intervals by selling
    Propter's Nicodemus Pills.

[IV]

Later, in his morning rambles
He perceived the moving brambles—
    Something square and white disclose;—
'Twas a First-class Railway-Ticket;

203

But, on stooping down to pick it
Off the ground,—a pea-green Cricket
    Settled on my uncle's Nose.

[v]

Never—never more,—oh! never,
Did that Cricket leave him ever,—
    Dawn or evening, day or night;—
Clinging as a constant treasure,—
Chirping with a cheerious measure,—
Wholly to my uncle's pleasure,—
    (Though his shoes were far too tight.)

[VI]

So for three-and-forty winters,
Till his shoes were worn to splinters,
    All those hills he wander'd o'er,—
Sometimes silent;—sometimes yelling;—
Till he came to Borley-Melling,
Near his old ancestral dwelling;—
    (But his shoes were far too tight.)

[VII]

On a little heap of Barley
Died my agèd uncle Arly,
    And they buried him one night;—
Close beside the leafy thicket;—
There,—his hat and Railway-Ticket;—
There,—his ever-faithful Cricket;—
    (But his shoes were far too tight.)

EDWARD LEAR

The Akond of Swat

Who, or why, or which, or *what*, Is the Akond of SWAT?
Is he tall or short, or dark or fair?
Does he sit on a stool or a sofa or chair,   or SQUAT,
       The Akond of Swat?

Is he wise or foolish, young or old?
Does he drink his soup and his coffee cold,   or HOT,
       The Akond of Swat?

Does he sing or whistle, jabber or talk,
And when riding abroad does he gallop or walk, or TROT,
       The Akond of Swat?

Does he wear a turban, a fez, or a hat?
Does he sleep on a mattress, a bed, or a mat,   or a COT,
       The Akond of Swat?

When he writes a copy in round-hand size,
Does he cross his T's and finish his I's   with a DOT,
       The Akond of Swat?

Can he write a letter concisely clear
Without a speck or a smudge or smear   or BLOT,
       The Akond of Swat?

Do his people like him extremely well?
Or do they, whenever they can, rebel,   or PLOT,
       At the Akond of Swat?

If he catches them then, either old or young,
Does he have them chopped in pieces or hung,   or *shot*,
       The Akond of Swat?

Do his people prig in the lanes or park?
Or even at times, when days are dark,   GAROTTE?
       O the Akond of Swat!

Does he study the wants of his own dominion?
Or doesn't he care for public opinion   a JOT,
       The Akond of Swat?

To amuse his mind do his people show him
Pictures, or any one's last new poem,   or WHAT,
                    For the Akond of Swat?

At night if he suddenly screams and wakes,
Do they bring him only a few small cakes,   or a LOT,
                    For the Akond of Swat?

Does he live on turnips, tea, or tripe?
Does he like his shawl to be marked with a stripe, or a DOT,
                    The Akond of Swat?

Does he like to lie on his back in a boat
Like the lady who lived in that isle remote,   SHALLOTT,
                    The Akond of Swat?

Is he quiet, or always making a fuss?
Is his steward a Swiss or a Swede or a Russ,   or a SCOT,
                    The Akond of Swat?

Does he like to sit by the calm blue wave?
Or to sleep and snore in a dark green cave,   or a GROTT,
                    The Akond of Swat?

Does he drink small beer from a silver jug?
Or a bowl? or a glass? or a cup? or a mug?   or a POT.
                    The Akond of Swat?

Does he beat his wife with a gold-topped pipe,
When she lets the gooseberries grow too ripe,   or ROT,
                    The Akond of Swat?

Does he wear a white tie when he dines with friends,
And tie it neat in a bow with ends,   or a KNOT,
                    The Akond of Swat?

Does he like new cream, and hate mince-pies?
When he looks at the sun does he wink his eyes, or NOT,
                    The Akond of Swat?

Does he teach his subjects to roast and bake?

Does he sàil about on an inland lake,   in a YACHT,
                                                    The Akond of Swat?

Some one, or nobody, knows I wot
Who or which or why or what

                                                Is the Akond of Swat!

EDWARD LEAR

The Mad Gardener's Song

He thought he saw an Elephant,
    That practised on a fife:
He looked again, and found it was
    A letter from his wife.
'At length I realise,' he said,
    'The bitterness of Life!'

He thought he saw a Buffalo
    Upon the chimney-piece:
He looked again, and found it was
    His Sister's Husband's Niece.
'Unless you leave this house,' he said,
    'I'll send for the Police!'

He thought he saw a Rattlesnake
    That questioned him in Greek:
He looked again, and found it was
    The Middle of Next Week.
'The one thing I regret,' he said,
    'Is that it cannot speak!'

He thought he saw a Banker's Clerk
    Descending from the bus:
He looked again, and found it was
    A Hippopotamus:
'If this should stay to dine,' he said,
    'There won't be much for us!'

207

He thought he saw a Kangaroo
  That worked a coffee-mill:
He looked again, and found it was
  A Vegetable-Pill.
'Were I to swallow this,' he said,
  'I should be very ill!'

He thought he saw a Coach-and-Four
  That stood beside his bed:
He looked again, and found it was
  A Bear without a Head.
'Poor thing,' he said, 'poor silly thing!
  It's waiting to be fed!'

He thought he saw an Albatross
  That fluttered round the lamp:
He looked again, and found it was
  A Penny-Postage-Stamp.
'You'd best be getting home,' he said:
  'The nights are very damp!'

He thought he saw a Garden-Door
  That opened with a key:
He looked again, and found it was
  A Double Rule of Three:
'And all its mystery,' he said,
  'Is clear as day to me!'

He thought he saw an Argument
  That proved he was the Pope:
He looked again, and found it was
  A Bar of Mottled Soap.
'A fact so dread,' he faintly said,
  'Extinguishes all hope!'

LEWIS CARROLL

The Three Badgers

There be three Badgers on a mossy stone
   Beside a dark and covered way:
Each dreams himself a monarch on his throne,
     And so they stay and stay—
Though their old Father languishes alone,
     They stay, and stay, and stay.

There be three Herrings loitering around,
   Longing to share that mossy seat:
Each Herring tries to sing what she has found
     That makes Life seem so sweet.
Thus, with a grating and uncertain sound,
     They bleat, and bleat, and bleat.

The Mother-Herring, on the salt sea-wave,
   Sought vainly for her absent ones:
The Father-Badger, writhing in a cave,
     Shrieked out 'Return, my sons!
You shall have buns,' he shrieked, 'if you'll behave!
     Yea, buns, and buns, and buns!'

'I fear,' said she, 'your sons have gone astray.
   My daughters left me while I slept.'
'Yes 'm,' the Badger said: 'it's as you say.
     They should be better kept.'
Thus the poor parents talked the time away,
     And wept, and wept, and wept.

'Oh, dear beyond our dearest dreams,
Fairer than all that fairest seems!
To feast the rosy hours away,
To revel in a roundelay!
     How blest would be
     A life so free—

Ipwergis-Pudding to consume,
And drink the subtle Azzigoom!

'And if, in other days and hours,
Mid other fluffs and other flowers,
The choice were given me how to dine—
"Name what thou wilt: it shall be thine!"
Oh, then I see
The life for me—
Ipwergis-Pudding to consume,
And drink the subtle Azzigoom!'

The Badgers did not care to talk to Fish:
They did not dote on Herrings' songs:
They never had experienced the dish
To which that name belongs:
'And oh, to pinch their tails,' (this was their wish,)
'With tongs, yea, tongs, and tongs!'

'And are not these the Fish,' the Eldest sighed,
'Whose Mother dwells beneath the foam?'
'They *are* the Fish!' the Second one replied.
'And they have left their home!'
'Oh, wicked Fish,' the Youngest Badger cried,
'To roam, yea, roam, and roam!'

Gently the Badgers trotted to the shore—
The sandy shore that fringed the bay:
Each in his mouth a living Herring bore—
Those aged ones waxed gay:
Clear rang their voices through the ocean's roar,
'Hooray, hooray, hooray!'

LEWIS CARROLL

The King-Fisher Song

King Fisher courted Lady Bird——
Sing Beans, sing Bones, sing Butterflies!
  'Find me my match,' he said,
  'With such a noble head——
With such a beard, as white as curd——
  With such expressive eyes!'

'Yet pins have heads,' said Lady Bird——
Sing Prunes, sing Prawns, sing Primrose-Hill!
  'And, where you stick them in,
  They stay, and thus a pin
Is very much to be preferred
  To one that's never still!'

'Oysters have beards,' said Lady Bird——
Sing Flies, sing Frogs, sing Fiddle-strings!
  'I love them, for I know
  They never chatter so:
They would not say one single word——
  Not if you crowned them Kings!'

'Needles have eyes,' said Lady Bird——
Sing Cats, sing Corks, sing Cowslip-tea!
  'And they are sharp—just what
  Your Majesty is *not*:
So get you gone—'tis too absurd
  To come a-courting *me*!'

LEWIS CARROLL

[*Tutor's Dignity*]

My one pupil has begun his work with me, and I will give you a description how the lecture is conducted. It is the most important point, you know, that the tutor should be *dignified* and at a distance from the pupil, and that the pupil should be as much as possible *degraded*.

Otherwise, you know, they are not humble enough.

So I sit at the further end of the room; outside the door (*which is shut*) sits the scout: outside the outer door (*also shut*) sits the sub-scout: half-way downstairs sits the sub-sub-scout; and down in the yard sits the *pupil*.

The questions are shouted from one to the other, and the answers come back in the same way—it is rather confusing till you are well used to it. The lecture goes on something like this:—

Tutor. What is twice three?
Scout. What's a rice tree?
Sub-Scout. When is ice free?
Sub-sub-Scout. What's a nice fee?
Pupil (timidly). Half a guinea!
Sub-sub-Scout. Can't forge any!
Sub-Scout. Ho for Jinny!
Scout. Don't be a ninny!
Tutor (looks offended, but tries another question). Divide a hundred by twelve!
Scout. Provide wonderful bells!
Sub-Scout. Go ride under it yourself!
Sub-sub-Scout. Deride the dunder-headed elf!
Pupi l (surprised). Who do you mean?
Sub-sub-Scout. Doings between!
Sub-Scout. Blue is the screen!
Scout. Soup-tureen!

And so the lecture proceeds.

LEWIS CARROLL

[Syzygy Chains]

PRISM
prismatic
dramatic
melodrama
melodious
ODIOUS
} Prove PRISM to be ODIOUS

DEMAND
eman
gentleman
gent
tangent
ange
orange
oran
CORMORANT
} DEMAND a CORMORANT

LEWIS CARROLL

Hit or Miss

*[Pairs of premises in search
of conclusions]*

No bald person needs a hair-brush;
No lizards have hair. }

No pins are ambitious;
No needles are pins. }

Some oysters are silent;
No silent creatures are amusing. }

No frogs write books;
Some people use ink in writing books. }

213

Some mountains are insurmountable; }
All stiles can be surmounted.

No lobsters are unreasonable; }
No reasonable creatures expect impossibilities. }

No fossil can be crossed in love; }
An oyster may be crossed in love. }

A prudent man shuns hyænas; }
No banker is imprudent. }

No misers are unselfish; }
None but misers save egg-shells. }

No military men write poetry; }
No generals are civilians. }

All owls are satisfactory; }
Some excuses are unsatisfactory. }

LEWIS CARROLL

[Lions and Gruel and Uncles]

Extract a Pair of Premises out of each of the following: and deduce the Conclusion, if there is one:—

'The Lion, as anyone can tell you who has been chased by them as often as *I* have, is a very savage animal; and there are certain individuals among them, though I will not guarantee it as a general law, who do not drink coffee.'

'It was most absurd of you to offer it! you might have known, if you had any sense, that no old sailors ever like gruel!'

'But I thought, as he was an uncle of yours—'
'An uncle of mine, indeed! Stuff!'
'You may call it stuff, if you like. All I know is, *my* uncles are all old men: and they like gruel like anything!'
'Well, then *your* uncles are—'

LEWIS CARROLL

[Fragment of a Song]

Lorenzo dwelt at Heighington,
  (Hys cote was made of Dimity,)
Least-ways yf not exactly there,
  Yet yn yt's close proximity.
Hee called on mee—hee stayed to tee—
  Yet not a word hee ut—tered,
Untyl I sayd, 'D'ye lyke your bread
Dry?' and hee answered 'But—tered.'

    (*Chorus*) Noodle dumb
           Has a noodle-head,
    I hate such noodles, *I* do.

LEWIS CARROLL

There was a young lady of station,
'I love man' was her sole exclamation;
    But when men cried, 'You flatter,'
    She replied, 'Oh! no matter,
Isle of Man is the true explanation.'

LEWIS CARROLL

The Little Man that had a Little Gun

In stature the Manlet was dwarfish—
  No burly big Blunderbore he:
And he wearily gazed on the crawfish
  His Wifelet had dressed for his tea.
'Now reach me, sweet Atom, my gunlet,
  And hurl the old shoelet for luck:
Let me hie to the bank of the runlet,
      And shoot thee a Duck!'

She has reached him his minikin gunlet:
  She has hurled the old shoelet for luck:
She is busily baking a bunlet,
  To welcome him home with his Duck.
On he speeds, never wasting a wordlet,
  Though thoughtlets cling, closely as wax,
To the spot where the beautiful birdlet
      So quietly quacks.

Where the Lobsterlet lurks, and the Crablet
  So slowly and sleepily crawls:
Where the Dolphin's at home, and the Dablet
  Pays long ceremonious calls:
Where the Grublet is sought by the Froglet:
  Where the Frog is pursued by the Duck:
Where the Ducklet is chased by the Doglet—
      So runs the world's luck!

He has loaded with bullet and powder:
  His footfall is noiseless as air:
But the Voices grow louder and louder,
  And bellow, and bluster, and blare.
They bristle before him and after,
  They flutter above and below,
Shrill shriekings of lubberly laughter,
      Weird wailings of woe!

They echo without him, within him:
  They thrill through his whiskers and beard:
Like a teetotum seeming to spin him,
  With sneers never hitherto sneered.
'Avengement,' they cry, 'on our Foelet!
  Let the Manikin weep for our wrongs!
Let us drench him, from toplet to toelet,
        With Nursery-Songs!

'He shall muse upon "Hey! Diddle! Diddle!"
  On the Cow that surmounted the Moon:
He shall rave of the Cat and the Fiddle,
  And the Dish that eloped with the Spoon:
And his soul shall be sad for the Spider,
  When Miss Muffet was sipping her whey,
That so tenderly sat down beside her,
        And scared her away!

'The music of Midsummer-madness
  Shall sting him with many a bite,
Till, in rapture of rollicking sadness,
  He shall groan with a gloomy delight:
He shall swathe him, like mists of the morning,
  In platitudes luscious and limp,
Such as deck, with a deathless adorning,
        The Song of the Shrimp!

'When the Ducklet's dark doom is decided,
  We will trundle him home in a trice:
And the banquet, so plainly provided,
  Shall round into rose-buds and rice:
In a blaze of pragmatic invention
  He shall wrestle with Fate, and shall reign:
But he has not a friend fit to mention,
        So hit him again!'

He has shot it, the delicate darling!
  And the Voices have ceased from their strife:

Not a whisper of sneering or snarling,
  As he carries it home to his wife:
Then, cheerily champing the bunlet
  His spouse was so skilful to bake,
He hies him once more to the runlet,
  To fetch her the Drake!

LEWIS CARROLL

Come into the orchard, Anne,
  For the dark owl, Night, has fled,
And Phosphor slumbers, as well as he can
  With a daffodil sky for a bed:
And the musk of the roses perplexes a man,
  And the pimpernel muddles his head.

A. C. SWINBURNE

Nephelidia

From the depth of the dreamy decline of the dawn
    through a notable nimbus of nebulous noonshine,
  Pallid and pink as the palm of the flag-flower that
    flickers with fear of the flies as they float,
Are they looks of our lovers that lustrously lean from
    a marvel of mystic miraculous moonshine,
  These that we feel in the blood of our blushes that
    thicken and threaten with throbs through the throat?
Thicken and thrill as a theatre thronged at appeal of
    an actor's appalled agitation,
  Fainter with fear of the fires of the future than pale
    with the promise of pride in the past;
Flushed with the famishing fullness of fever that
    reddens with radiance of rathe recreation,
  Gaunt as the ghastliest of glimpses that gleam
    through the gloom of the gloaming when ghosts
    go aghast?

Nay, for the nick of the tick of the time is a tremulous
    touch on the temples of terror,
  Strained as the sinews yet strenuous with strife of
    the dead who is dumb as the dust-heaps of death:
Surely no soul is it, sweet as the spasm of erotic emotional
    exquisite error,
  Bathed in the balms of beatified bliss, beatific itself
    by beatitude's breath.
Surely no spirit or sense of a soul that was soft to the
    spirit and soul of our senses
  Sweetens the stress of suspiring supicion that sobs
    in the semblance and sound of a sigh;
Only this oracle opens Olympian, in mystical moods
    and triangular tenses—
  'Life is the lust of a lamp for the light that is dark
    till the dawn of the day when we die.'
Mild is the mirk and monotonous music of memory,
    melodiously mute as it may be,
  While the hope in the heart of a hero is bruised by
    the breach of men's rapiers, resigned to the rod;
Made meek as a mother whose bosom-beats bound with
    the bliss-bringing bulk of a balm-breathing baby,
  As they grope through the grave-yard of creeds,
    under skies growing green at a groan for the
    grimness of God.
Blank is the book of his bounty beholden of old, and
    its binding is blacker than bluer:
  Out of blue into black is the scheme of the skies, and
    their dews are the wine of the bloodshed of things;
Till the darkling desire of delight shall be free as a
    fawn that is freed from the fangs that pursue her,
  Till the heart-beats of hell shall be hushed by a hymn
    from the hunt that has harried the kennel of kings.

A. C. SWINBURNE

The Higher Pantheism in a Nutshell

One, who is not, we see: but one, whom we see not,
  is:
Surely this is not that: but that is assuredly this.

What, and wherefore, and whence? for under is over
  and under:
If thunder could be without lightning, lightning could
  be without thunder.

Doubt is faith in the main: but faith, on the whole,
  is doubt:
We cannot believe by proof: but could we believe
  without?

Why, and whither, and how? for barley and rye are
  not clover:
Neither are straight lines curves: yet over is under
  and over.

Two and two may be four: but four and four are not
  eight:
Fate and God may be twain: but God is the same
  thing as fate.

Ask a man what he thinks, and get from a man what
  he feels:
God, once caught in the fact, shows you a fair pair
  of heels.

Body and spirit are twins: God only knows which is
  which:
The soul squats down in the flesh, like a tinker drunk
  in a ditch.

More is the whole than a part: but half is more than
    the whole:
Clearly, the soul is the body: but is not the body the
    soul?

One and two are not one: but one and nothing is
    two:
Truth can hardly be false, if falsehood cannot be
    true.

Once the mastodon was: pterodactyls were common
    as cocks:
Then the mammoth was God: now is He a prize ox.

Parallels all things are: yet many of these are askew:
You are certainly I: but certainly I am not you.

Springs the rock from the plain, shoots the stream
    from the rock:
Cocks exist for the hen: but hens exist for the cock.

God, whom we see not, is: and God, who is not, we
    see:
Fiddle, we know, is diddle: and diddle, we take it,
    is dee.

A. C. SWINBURNE

Select Spoonerisms

*(manufactured in Oxford and fathered on William Archibald Spooner,
for thirteen years Dean, and later Warden, of New College)*

In a sermon in New College chapel: 'Yes, Our Lord is indeed
a shoving leopard.'

221

Announcing the hymns in chapel: 'Hymn 175, Kinquering Congs their titles take.'

In another college sermon: 'Which of us has not felt in his heart a half-warmed fish?'

At the optician's:
> 'Have you a signifying glass?'
> 'A what, sir?'
> 'A signifying glass.'
> 'I don't think we stock them, sir.'
> 'Oh well, it doesn't magnify.'

Proposing a toast: 'Let us drink to the queer old Dean.'

To a former undergraduate: 'I remember your name perfectly, but I just cannot think of your face.'

To a defaulting undergraduate: 'Sir, you have tasted a whole worm. You have hissed my mystery lectures. You were fighting a liar in the quadrangle. You will leave Oxford by the town drain.'

ANON

Little Birds

Little Birds are dining
> Warily and well
> Hid in mossy cell:
Hid, I say, by waiters
Gorgeous in their gaiters—
> I've a Tale to tell.

Little Birds are feeding
> Justices with jam,
> Rich in frizzled ham:
Rich, I say, in oysters—

Haunting shady cloisters—
    That is what I am.

Little Birds are teaching
    Tigresses to smile,
    Innocent of guile:
Smile, I say, not smirkle—
Mouth a semicircle,
    That's the proper style!

Little Birds are sleeping
    All among the pins,
    Where the loser wins:
Where, I say, he sneezes,
When and how he pleases—
    So the Tale begins.

Little Birds are writing
    Interesting books,
    To be read by cooks;
Read, I say, not roasted—
Letterpress, when toasted,
    Loses its good looks.

Little Birds are seeking
    Hecatombs of haws,
    Dressed in snowy gauze:
Dressed, I say, in fringes
Half-alive with hinges—
    Thus they break the laws.

Little Birds are playing
    Bagpipes on the shore,
    Where the tourists snore:
'Thanks!' they cry. ' 'Tis thrilling.
Take, oh, take this shilling!
    Let us have no more!'

Little Birds are bathing
        Crocodiles in cream,
        Like a happy dream:
Like, but not so lasting—
Crocodiles, when fasting,
        Are not all they seem!

Little Birds are choking
        Baronets with bun,
        Taught to fire a gun:
Taught, I say, to splinter
Salmon in the winter—
        Merely for the fun.

Little Birds are hiding
        Crimes in carpet-bags,
        Blessed by happy stags:
Blessed, I say, though beaten—
Since our friends are eaten
        When the memory flags.

Little Birds are tasting
        Gratitude and gold,
        Pale with sudden cold;
Pale, I say, and wrinkled—
When the bells have tinkled,
        And the Tale is told.

LEWIS CARROLL

Le Hareng Saur

Il était un grand mur blanc—nu, nu, nu,
Contre le mur une échelle—haute, haute, haute,
Et, par terre, un hareng saur—sec, sec, sec.

Il vient, tenant dans ses mains—sales, sales, sales,
Un marteau lourd, un grand clou—pointu, pointu, pointu,
Un peloton de ficelle—gros, gros, gros.

Alors il monte à l'échelle—haute, haute, haute,
Et plante le clou pointu—toc, toc, toc,
Tout en haut du grand mur blanc—nu, nu, nu.

Il laisse aller le marteau—qui tombe, qui tombe, qui tombe,
Attache au clou la ficelle—longue, longue, longue,
Et, au bout le hareng saur—sec, sec, sec.

Il redescend de l'échelle—haute, haute, haute,
L'emporte avec le marteau—lourd, lourd, lourd,
Et puis, il s'en va ailleurs—loin, loin, loin.

Et, depuis, le hareng saur—sec, sec, sec.
Au bout de cette ficelle—longue, longue, longue,
Très lentement se balance—toujours, toujours, toujours.

J'ai composé cette histoire,—simple, simple, simple,
Pour mettre en fureur les gens—graves, graves, graves,
Et amuser les enfants—petits, petits, petits.

CHARLES CROS

Chanson de la Côte

Voici rentrer l'officier de marine,
        Il a de noirs favoris.
Le vent de mer a gonflé sa narine,
Il dit combien de vaisseaux il a pris.

Voici rentrer l'officier de marine,
        Il a deux beaux galons d'or.
Il veut surprendre, au logis, Mathurine
Sa femme, son plus précieux trésor.

Voici rentrer l'officier de marine,
   Il veut revoir sa maison,
Son lard qui sèche et ses sacs de farine,
Ses pommiers lourds de pommes à foison.

Repars bien vite, officier de marine,
   Tes pommiers on a coupé,
Tes sacs vidés, ton lard frit. Mathurine
Avec des gens de terre t'a trompé.

Repars bien vite, officier de marine,
   Pour un voyage bien long.
Tes favoris seront blancs, ta narine
Sera ridée au troisième galon.

CHARLES CROS

The Pessimist

Nothing to do but work,
   Nothing to eat but food,
Nothing to wear but clothes,
   To keep one from going nude.

Nothing to breathe but air,
   Quick as a flash 'tis gone;
Nowhere to fall but off,
   Nowhere to stand but on.

Nothing to comb but hair,
   Nowhere to sleep but in bed,
Nothing to weep but tears,
   Nothing to bury but dead.

Nothing to sing but songs,
   Ah, well, alas! alack!

Nowhere to go but out,
   Nowhere to come but back.

Nothing to see but sights,
   Nothing to quench but thirst,
Nothing to have but what we've got.
   Thus thro' life we are cursed.

Nothing to strike but a gait;
   Everything moves that goes.
Nothing at all but common sense
   Can ever withstand these woes.

BENJAMIN FRANKLIN KING

The Undertaker's Horse

'To-tschin-shu is condemned to death. How can he drink tea with the Executioner?'—*Japanese Proverb*

The eldest son bestrides him,
And the pretty daughter rides him,
And I meet him oft o' mornings on the Course;
And there kindles in my bosom
An emotion chill and gruesome
As I canter past the Undertaker's Horse.

Neither shies he nor is restive,
But a hideously suggestive
Trot, professional and placid, he affects;
And the cadence of his hoof-beats
To my mind this grim reproof beats:—
'Mend your pace, my friend, I'm coming. Who's the next?'

Ah! stud-bred of ill-omen,
I have watched the strongest go—men

Of pith and might and muscle—at your heels,
Down the plantain-bordered highway,
(Heaven send it ne'er by my way!)
In a lacquered box and jetty upon wheels.

Answer, sombre beast and dreary,
Where is Brown, the young, the cheery,
Smith, the pride of all his friends and half the Force?
You were at that last dread *dak**
We must cover at a walk,
Bring them back to me, O Undertaker's Horse!

With your mane unhogged and flowing,
And your curious way of going,
And that businesslike black crimping of your tail,
E'en with Beauty on your back, Sir,
Pacing as a lady's hack, Sir,
What wonder when I meet you I turn pale?

It may be you wait your time, Beast,
Till I write my last bad rhyme, Beast—
Quit the sunlight, cut the rhyming, drop the glass—
Follow after with the others,
Where some dusky heathen smothers
Us with marigolds in lieu of English grass.

Or, perchance, in years to follow,
I shall watch your plump sides hollow,
See Carnifex (gone lame) become a corse—
See old age at last o'erpower you,
And the Station Pack devour you,
I shall chuckle then, O Undertaker's Horse!

But to insult, jibe, and quest, I've
Still the hideously suggestive

* Stage of a journey

Trot that hammers out the unrelenting text,
And I hear it hard behind me
In what place soe'er I find me:—
' 'Sure to catch you sooner or later. Who's the next?'

RUDYARD KIPLING

The Boy of Quebec

There was a young boy of Quebec,
Who fell into the ice to his neck.
　　When asked 'Are you friz?'
　　He replied 'Yes, I is,
But we don't call this cold in Quebec.'

?RUDYARD KIPLING

A Woman's Reason

I'm sure every word that you say is absurd;
　I say it's all gummidge and twaddle;
You may argue away till the 19th. of May,
　But I don't like the sound of the moddle.

GELETT BURGESS

Remarkable Art

Remarkable
　Truly is Art!
See—elliptical
　Wheels on a cart!
It looks very fair

In the picture, up there,
But imagine the
    Ride, when you start.

GELETT BURGESS

Trapping fairies in West Virginia
I think I never saw fairies skinnier.

GELETT BURGESS

A Radical Creed

I don't give a $\sqrt{D^2}$
For the stuff you denominate hair
And your fingers and toes and your
    Neck and your nose,
These are things it revolts me to wear.

GELETT BURGESS

There was a young man of Montrose
Who had pockets in none of his clothes.
    When asked by his lass
    Where he carried his brass,
He said: 'Darling, I pay through the nose.'

ARNOLD BENNETT

On Drawing-room Amenities

There is little in afternoon tea
To appeal to a person like me;
Polite conversation evokes the elation
   A cow might enjoy in a tree.

GELETT BURGESS

[The Shades of Night]

The shades of night were falling fast,
   And the rain was falling faster,
When through an Alpine village passed
   An Alpine village pastor:
A youth who bore mid snow and ice
   A bird that wouldn't chirrup,
And a banner with the strange device—
   'Mrs. Winslow's soothing syrup'.

'Beware the pass', the old man said,
   'My bold, my desperate fellah;
Dark lowers the tempest overhead,
   And you'll want your umberella;
And the roaring torrent is deep and wide—
   You may hear how loud it washes.'
But still that clarion voice replied:
   'I've got my old goloshes.'

'Oh, stay', the maiden said, 'and rest
   (For the wind blows from the nor'ward)
Thy weary head upon my breast—
   And please don't think I'm forward.'

A tear stood in his bright blue eye,
  And he gladly would have tarried;
But still he answered with a sigh:
  'Unhappily I'm married.'

A. E. HOUSMAN

The Song Called
'His Hide is Covered with Hair'

The dog is a faithful, intelligent friend,
  But his hide is covered with hair;
The cat will inhabit the house to the end,
  But *her* hide is covered with hair.

The hide of the mammoth was covered with wool,
The hide of the porpoise is sleek and cool,
But you'll find, if you look at that gambolling fool,
  That his hide is covered with hair.

Oh, I thank my God for this at the least,
I was born in the West and not in the East,
And He made me a human instead of a beast,
  Whose hide is covered with hair!

The cow in the pasture that chews the cud,
  Her hide is covered with hair.
And even a horse of the Barbary blood,
  His hide is covered with hair!

The camel excels in a number of ways,
And travellers give him unlimited praise—
He can go without drinking for several days—
  But his hide is covered with hair.

The bear of the forest that lives in a pit,
   His hide is covered with hair;
The laughing hyena in spite of his wit,
   His hide is covered with hair!

The Barbary ape and the chimpanzee,
And the lion of Africa, verily he,
With his head like a wig, and the tuft on his knee,
   His hide . . .

HILAIRE BELLOC

Lord Abbott

Lord Abbott's coronet was far too small,
So small, that as he sauntered down Whitehall
Even the youthful Proletariat
(Who probably mistook it for a Hat)
Remarked on its exiguous extent.
There is a picture of the incident.

HILAIRE BELLOC

Marezle toats,
Dozle toats.
Dozle tivy-too

ANON

Infant Innocence

Reader, behold! this monster wild
Has gobbled up the infant child.
The infant child is not aware
It has been eaten by the bear.

A. E. HOUSMAN

[G. K. Chesterton on his Birth]

When I was born in a world of sin,
Praise be God it was raining gin;
Gin on the house, gin on the walls,
Gin on the bun-shops and copy-book stalls.

A. E. HOUSMAN

Amelia mixed the mustard,
    She mixed it good and thick;
She put it in the custard
    And made her Mother sick,
And showing satisfaction
    By many a loud huzza
'Observe' said she 'the action
    Of mustard on Mamma.'

A. E. HOUSMAN

Mr. Ody met a body
Hanging from a tree;
And what was worse
He met a hearse
As black as black could be.
Mr. Ody said 'By God, he
Ought to have a ride.'
Said the driver 'I'd oblige yer,
But we're full inside.'

EDITH NESBIT

234

On the Death of a Female Officer
of the Salvation Army

'Hallelujah!' was the only observation
That escaped Lieutenant-Colonel Mary Jane,
When she tumbled off the platform in the station,
And was cut in little pieces by the train.
  Mary Jane, the train is through yer,
  Hallelujah, Hallelujah!
We will gather up the fragments that remain.

A. E. HOUSMAN

Profoundly True Reflections on the Sea

O billows bounding far,
How wet, how wet ye are!

When first my gaze you met
I said 'These waves are wet.'

I said it, and am quite
Convinced that I was right.

Who saith that ye are dry?
I give that man the lie.

Thy wetness, O thou sea,
Is wonderful to me.

It agitates my heart,
To think how wet thou art.

No object I have met
Is more profoundly wet.

Methinks 'twere vain to try,
O sea, to wipe thee dry.

I therefore will refrain.
Farewell, thou humid main.

A. E. HOUSMAN

Four Poems

The Purple Cow
I never saw a Purple Cow,
I never hope to see one;
But I can tell you, anyhow,
I'd rather see than be one.

Parisian Nectar
Many people seem to think
    Plaster of Paris
    Good to drink;
Though conducive unto quiet.
I prefer another diet.

The Sunset
The sun is low, to say the least,
  Although it is well-red;
Yet, since it rises in the yeast,
  It should be better bred.

Confession
Ah, yes! I wrote the 'Purple Cow'—
  I'm sorry, now, I wrote it,
But I can tell you anyhow,
  I'll kill you if you quote it.

GELETT BURGESS

Hexameter and Pentameter

Down in a deep dark ditch sat an old cow munching a
  beanstalk.
Out of her mouth came forth strawberry, strawberry froth.

ANON

Archbishop Tait

There was an Archbishop named Tait
Who dined with a friend at 8.8.
  I regret to relate
  I'm unable to state
What Tait's tête-à-tête ate at 8.8.

ANON

Sonnet for a Picture

That nose is out of drawing. With a gasp,
  She pants upon the passionate lips that ache
  With the red drain of her own mouth, and make
A monochord of colour. Like an asp,
One lithe lock wriggles in his rutilant grasp.
  Her bosom is an oven of myrrh, to bake
  Love's white warm shewbread to a browner cake.
The lock his fingers clench has burst its hasp.
The legs are absolutely abominable.
  Ah! what keen overgust of wild-eyed woes
  Flags in that bosom, flushes in that nose?
Nay! Death sets riddles for desire to spell,
  Responsive. What red hem earth's passion sews,
But may be ravenously unripped in hell?

A. C. SWINBURNE

At the Piano

[I]

Love me and leave me; what love bids retrieve me?
    can June's fist grasp May?
Leave me and love me; hopes eyed once above me
    like spring's sprouts decay;
Fall as the snow falls, when summer leaves grow
    false—cards packed for storm's play!

[II]

Nay, say Decay's self be but last May's elf, wing
    shifted, eye sheathe—
Changeling in April's crib rocked, who lets 'scape
    rills locked fast since frost breathed—
Skin cast (think!) adder-like, now bloom bursts
    bladder-like,—bloom frost bequeathed?

[III]

Ah, how can fear sit and hear as love hears it grief's
    heart's cracked grate's screech?
Chance lets the gate sway that opens on hate's way
    and shews on shame's beach
Crouched like an imp sly change watch sweet love's
    shrimps lie, a toothful in each.

[IV]

Time feels his tooth slip on husks wet from Truth's
    lip, which drops them and grins—
Shells where no throb stirs of life left in lobsters
    since joy thrilled their fins—
Hues of the prawn's tail or comb that makes dawn
    stale, so red for our sins!

[V]

Years blind and deaf use the soul's joys as refuse,
    heart's peace as manure,

Reared whence, next June's rose shall bloom where
  our moons rose last year, just as pure:
Moons' ends match roses' ends: men by beasts'
  noses' ends mete sin's stink's cure.

[VI]

Leaves love last year smelt now feel dead love's tears
  melt—flies caught in time's mesh!
Salt are the dews in which new time breeds new sin,
  brews blood and stews flesh;
Next year may see dead more germs than this weeded
  and reared them afresh.

[VII]

Old times left perish, there's new time to cherish;
  life just shifts its tune;
As, when the day dies, earth, half afraid, eyes the
  growth of the moon;
Love me and save me, take me or waive me; death
  takes one so soon!

A. C. SWINBURNE

Miss Ellen Gee of Kew

Peerless yet hopeless maid of Q,
  Accomplish'd L N G,
Never again shall I and U
  Together sip our T.
For oh! the fates, I know not Y,
  Sent 'midst the flowers a B;
Which ven'mous stung her in the I,
  So that she could not C.
    L N exclaimed, 'Vile spiteful B,
      If ever I catch U
    On jessmine, rosebud or sweet P,
      I'll change your singing Q.

239

'I'll send you like a lamb or U,
    Across the Atlantic C;
From our delightful village Q,
    To distant O Y E.
A stream runs from my wounded I,
    Salt as the briny C,
As rapid as the X or Y,
    The O I O or D.

'Then fare thee ill, insensate B,
    Which stung nor yet knew Y,
Since not for wealthy Durham's C
    Would I have lost my I.'
They bear with tears poor L N G
    In funeral R A,
A clay cold corpse now doomed to B,
    Whilst I mourn her D K.

Ye nymphs of Q, then shun each B,
    List to the reason Y;
For should A B C U at T,
    He'll surely sting your I.
Now in a grave L deep in Q,
    She's cold as cold can B;
Whilst robins sing upon A U,
    Her dirge and L E G.

    L N exclaimed, 'Vile spiteful B,
        If ever I catch U
    On jessmine, rosebud or sweet P,
        I'll change your singing Q.'

ANON

On the Motor Bus

What is this that roareth thus?
Can it be a Motor Bus?
Yes, the smell and hideous hum
Indicat Motorem Bum!
Implet in the Corn and High
Terror me Motoris Bi:
Bo Motori clamitabo
Ne Motore caedar a Bo—
Dative be or Ablative
So thou only let us live:—
Whither shall thy victims flee?
Spare us, spare us, Motor Be!
Thus I sang; and still anigh
Came in hordes Motores Bi,
Et complebat omne forum
Copia Motorum Borum.
How shall wretches live like us
Cincti Bis Motoribus?
Domine, defende nos
Contra hos Motores Bos!

A. D. GODLEY

Fragment of a Greek Tragedy

CHORUS: O suitably-attired-in-leather-boots
Head of a traveler, wherefore seeking whom
Whence by what way how purposed art thou come
To this well-nightingaled vicinity?
My object in inquiring is to know.
But if you happen to be deaf and dumb
And do not understand a word I say,
Then wave your hand, to signify as much.

ALC: I journeyed hither a Boetian road.
CHORUS: Sailing on horseback, or with feet for oars?
ALC: Plying with speed my partnership of legs.
CHORUS: Beneath a shining or a rainy Zeus?
ALC: Mud's sister, not himself, adorns my shoes.
CHORUS: To learn your name would not displease me much.
ALC: Not all that men desire do they obtain.
CHORUS: Might I then hear at what your presence shoots?
ALC: A shepherd's questioned mouth informed me that—
CHORUS: What? for I know not yet what you will say.
ALC: Nor will you ever, if you interrupt.
CHORUS: Proceed, and I will hold my speechless tongue.
ALC: This house was Eriphyla's, no one's else.
CHORUS: Nor did he shame his throat with shameful lies.
ALC: May I then enter, passing through the door?
CHORUS: Go chase into the house a lucky foot.
    And, O my son, be, on the one hand, good,
    And do not, on the other hand, be bad;
    For that is very much the safest plan.
ALC: I go into the house with heels and speed.

CHORUS:
    Strophe

    In speculation
    I would not willingly acquire a name
        For ill-digested thought;
        But after pondering much
    To this conclusion I at last have come:
        Life is uncertain.
        This truth I have written deep
        In my reflective midriff
        On tablets not of wax,
    Nor with a pen did I inscribe it there,
    For many reasons: *Life*, I say, *is not*
        A stranger to uncertainty.
    Not from the flight of omen-yelling fowls

242

    This fact did I discover,
Nor did the Delphine tripod bark it out,
    Nor yet Dodona.
Its native ingenuity sufficed
    My self-taught diaphragm.

Antistrophe

    Why should I mention
The Inachean daughter, loved of Zeus?
    Her whom of old the gods,
    More provident than kind,
Provided with four hoofs, two horns, one tail,
    A gift not asked for,
    And sent her forth to learn
    The unfamiliar science
    Of how to chew the cud.
She therefore, all about the Argive fields,
Went cropping pale green grass and nettle-tops,
    Nor did they disagree with her.
But yet, howe'er nutritious, such repasts
    I do not hanker after:
Never may Cypris for her seat select
    My dappled liver!
Why should I mention Io? Why indeed?
    I have no notion why.

Epode

    But now does my boding heart,
    Unhired, unaccompanied, sing
    A strain not meet for the dance.
    Yea even the palace appears
    To my yoke of circular eyes
    (The right, nor omit I the left)
    Like a slaughterhouse, so to speak,
    Garnished with woolly deaths

And many shipwrecks of cows.
I therefore in a Cissian strain lament;
    And to the rapid
    Loud, linen-tattering thumps upon my chest
    Resounds in concert
The battering of my unlucky head.
ERI (*within*): O, I am smitten with a hatchet's jaw;
    And that in deed and not in word alone.
CHORUS: I thought I heard a sound within the house
    Unlike the voice of one that jumps for joy.
ERI: He splits my skull, not in a friendly way,
    Once more: he purposes to kill me dead
CHORUS: I would not be reputed rash, but yet
    I doubt if all be gay within the house.
ERI: O! O! another stroke! that makes the third.
    He stabs me to the heart against my wish.
CHORUS: If that be so, thy state of health is poor;
    But thine arithmetic is quite correct.

A. E. HOUSMAN

See, Will, 'Ere's a Go

Civile, res ago,
Fortibus es in ero.
Gnoses mare, Thebe trux.
Vatis inem?
Causan dux.

ANON

Song of Duke William

Duke William was a wench's son,
His grandfer was a tanner!

244

He drank his cider from the tun,
  Which is the Norman manner:
His throne was made of oak and gold,
  His bow-shaft of the yew—
That is the way the tale is told,
  I doubt if it be true!

  But what care I for him?
  My tankard is full to the brim,
  And I'll sing Elizabeth, Dorothy,
    Margaret, Mary, Dorinda, Persephone, Miriam,
  Pegotty taut and trim.

The men that sailed to Normandy
  Foul weather may they find;
For banging about in the waist of a ship
  Was never to my mind.
They drink their rum in the glory-hole
  In quaking and in fear;
But a better man was left behind,
  And he sits drinking beer.

  But what care I for the swine?
  They never were fellows of mine!
  And I'll sing Elizabeth, Dorothy,
    Margaret, Mary, Dorinda,
    Persephone, Miriam, Pegotty,
    Jezebel, Topsy, Andromeda,
    Magdalen, Emily, Charity, Agatha, Beatrice,
      Anna, Cecilia, Maud, Cleopatra, Selene,
      and Jessica . . .
              Barbara stout and fine.

                    HILAIRE BELLOC

245

Henry King who Chewed Bits of String, and was Early Cut off in Dreadful Agonies

The Chief Defect of Henry King
  Was chewing little bits of String.
At last he swallowed some which tied
  Itself in ugly Knots inside.
Physicians of the Utmost Fame
Were called at once; but when they came
They answered, as they took their Fees,
'There is no Cure for this Disease.
Henry will very soon be dead.'
His Parents stood about his Bed
Lamenting his Untimely Death,
When Henry, with his Latest Breath,
Cried—'Oh, my Friends, be warned by me,
That Breakfast, Dinner, Lunch, and Tea
Are all the Human Frame requires . . . .'
With that, the Wretched Child expires.

HILAIRE BELLOC

[O Have you Caught the Tiger]

O have you caught the tiger?
  And can you hold him tight?
And what immortal hand or eye
Could frame his fearful symmetry?
  And does he try to bite?

Yes, I have caught the tiger,
  And he was hard to catch.
O tiger, tiger, do not try

To put your tail into my eye,
    And do not bite and scratch.

Yes, I have caught the tiger.
    O tiger, do not bray!
And what immortal hand or eye
Could frame his fearful symmetry
    I should not like to say.

And may I see the tiger?
    I should indeed delight
To see so large an animal
Without a voyage to Bengal.
    And mind you hold him tight.

Yes, you may see the tiger;
    It will amuse you much.
The tiger is, as you will find,
A creature of the feline kind.
    And mind you do not touch.

And do you feed the tiger,
    And do you keep him clean?
He has a less contented look
Than in the Natural History book,
    And seems a trifle lean.

Oh yes, I feed the tiger,
    And soon he will be plump;
I give him groundsel fresh and sweet,
And much canary-seed to eat,
    And wash him at the pump.

It seems to me the tiger
　　Has not been lately fed,
Not for a day or two at least;
And that is why the noble beast
　　Has bitten off your head.

A. E. HOUSMAN

The Funnels

A pair of funnels stroll by night. They both
collect inside themselves the white moon-
light, so clear, so calm, so bright,
which then runs down the runnels
of these funnels, making
their woodland way
much brighter,
und so
weit-
er.

CHRISTIAN MORGENSTERN
(tr. Geoffrey Grigson)

The Great Lalulā

Kroklokwafzi? Seṁememi!
Seiokrontro—prafriplo:
Bifzi, bafzi; hulalemi:
quasti basti bo . . .
Lalu lalu lalu lalu la!

Hontraruru miromente
zasku zes rü rü?

Entepente, leiolente
klekwapufzi lü?
lalu lalu lalu lalu la!

Simarar kos malzipempu
silzuzankunkrei (;)!
Marjomar dos: Quempu Lempu
Siri Suri Sei [ ]!
Lalu lalu lalu lalu la!

CHRISTIAN MORGENSTERN

Philosophy is Born

The moorland sheep is frightened and amazed
At seeing me. What can this mean?
It means I might be the first man this sheep has ever seen.
An infectious gaze, we stand and stare as if we were asleep.
I might in fact be seeing my first sheep.

CHRISTIAN MORGENSTERN
(tr. Geoffrey Grigson)

Korf's Clock

Two pairs of hands go round
on a clock Korf's made
to indicate time advancing,
and time retrograde.

Ten and two it says at once,
it says both three and nine,
and everyone who looks at it
loses his fear of time,

249

for on this Janus-clock
of Korf's ingenious design
time (as Korf intended)
neutralizes time.

CHRISTIAN MORGENSTERN
(tr. Geoffrey Grigson)

The Moonsheep

The Moonsheep on the wide plain stands.
He waits for the Great Shearer's hands.
    The Moonsheep.

The Moonsheep nibbles a rhizome,
And goes back to his alpine home.
    The Moonsheep.

The Moonsheep in a dream says he
Is Space's dark Infinity.
    The Moonsheep.

The Moonsheep in the dawn lies dead.
'His body's white, the sun is red.
    The Moonsheep.

CHRISTIAN MORGENSTERN
(tr. Geoffrey Grigson)

Lunovis

Lunovis in planitie stat
Cultrumque magn' expectitat.
    Lunovis.

Lunovis herba rapta it
In montes, unde cucurrit.
            Lunovis.

Lunovis habet somnium:
Se culmen rer' ess' omnium.
            Lunovis.

Lunovis mane mortuumst.
Sol ruber atque ips' albumst.
            Lunovis.

CHRISTIAN MORGENSTERN

The Camelopard

The Camelopard, it is said
    By travellers (who never lie),
He cannot stretch out straight in bed
    Because he is so high.
The clouds surround his lofty head,
    His hornlets touch the sky.

How shall I hunt this quadruped?
    I cannot tell! Not I!
I'll buy a little parachute
    (A common parachute with wings),
I'll fill it full of arrowroot
    And other necessary things,

And I will slay this fearful brute
With stones and sticks and guns and slings.

HILAIRE BELLOC

[Various Beasts]

The Llama

The Llama is a woolly sort of fleecy hairy goat,
With an indolent expression and an undulating throat
   Like an unsuccessful literary man.
And I know the place he lives in (or at least—I think I do)
It is Ecuador, Brazil or Chile—possibly Peru;
   You must find it in the Atlas if you can.
The Llama of the Pampasses you never should confound
(In spite of a deceptive similarity of sound)
   With the Lama who is Lord of Turkestan.
For the former is a beautiful and valuable beast,
But the latter is not lovable nor useful in the least;
And the Ruminant is preferable surely to the Priest
Who battens on the woful superstitions of the East,
   The Mongol of the Monastery of Shan.

The Chamois

   The Chamois inhabits
   Lucerne, where his habits
      (Though why I have not an idea-r)
   Give him sudden short spasms
   On the brink of deep chasms,
      And he lives in perpetual fear.

The Bison

   The Bison is vain, and (I write it with pain)
      The Door-mat you see on his head
   Is not, as some learned professors maintain,
   The opulent growth of a genius' brain;
      But is sewn on with needle and thread.

The Viper

Yet another great truth I record in my verse,
That some Vipers are venomous, some the reverse;

A fact you may prove if you try,
By procuring two Vipers, and letting them bite;
With the *first* you are only the worse for a fright,
    But after the *second* you die.

The Hippopotamus
I shoot the Hippopotamus
With bullets made of platinum,
Because if I use leaden ones
His hide is sure to flatten 'em.

G stands for Gnu, whose weapons of Defence
Are long, sharp, curling Horns, and Common-sense.
To these he adds a Name so short and strong
That even Hardy Boers pronounce it wrong.
How often on a bright Autumnal day
The Pious people of Pretoria say,
'Come, let us hunt the—' Then no more is heard
But Sounds of Strong Men struggling with a word.
Meanwhile, the distant Gnu with grateful eyes
Observes his opportunity, and flies.

MORAL
Child, if you have a rummy kind of name,
Remember to be thankful for the same.

HILAIRE BELLOC

The Salmon

To Switzerland, right up the Rhine,
A Salmon swam.

He managed one by one each
Salmon-dam.

Up, up he went, to God knows where,
And there,

Twelve feet or more above him, rose
A weir.

Ten feet he jumped, so well, and fell.
Dismayed,

Below that Alp three
Weeks he stayed,

And then turned round at last
And swam,

In silence, back to Amst-
-Erdam.

CHRISTIAN MORGENSTERN
(tr. Geoffrey Grigson)

On the Planet of Flies

On the Planet of Flies
it's a poor show for men.
What they do here to flies
flies there do to them.

Men find themselves sticking
on man-papers there,
or swim round and sink
in sugar and beer.

On some points I give
the prize to the flies,

we're not mistakenly swallowed
or cooked in their pies.

CHRISTIAN MORGENSTERN
(tr. Geoffrey Grigson)

The Aesthete Weasel

A Weasel (or a Stoat)
sat afloat on a clote
in the moat.

Why?

The Mooncalf,
off the record, gave me
this reply:

this aesthete-creat-
ure sat there
all
that time
for
Rhyme.

CHRISTIAN MORGENSTERN
(tr. Geoffrey Grigson)

The Knee on Its Own

A lone knee wanders through the world,
    A knee and nothing more;
It's not a tent, it's not a tree,
    A knee and nothing more.

In battle once there was a man
  Shot foully through and through;
The knee alone remained unhurt
  As saints are said to do.

Since then it's wandered through the world,
  A knee and nothing more.
It's not a tent, it's not a tree,
  A knee and nothing more.

CHRISTIAN MORGENSTERN
(tr. R. F. C. Hull)

Eli the Thatcher

O thou whose name shatters the universe,
Eli, old thatcher who in long-gone days
Thatched other heads than mine, whose puny verse
Totters along like an old man in stays.
What stories of these hills hast thou to tell!
Stories of sheep that turned their fangs on men,
Of rabbits that could cast their awful spell
Even on poachers and two-headed calves!
Tell us some story now, to rouse our blood,
Of that old Squire whose son you cut in halves,
Of ladies roasted, babies cooked in mud—
Come, greybeard, rouse yourself, and let none say
You have forgot to tread the ancient way.

MAX BEERBOHM and WILLIAM ROTHENSTEIN
(Even lines by Beerbohm, odd lines
by Rothenstein)

The Road to Zoagli

(*Ligurian Folk Song*)

[saved at the last moment by Cecil Max Beerbohm Sharp]

Have ye seen the would-be-not-humble dandy,
    With his long black cloak and his short trousers grey?
I saw him, dear heart, this morn as ever was, on the
                              road to Zoagli,
    And I looked the other way.

What said the would-be-not-humble dandy,
    With his long black cloak and his short trousers grey?
He said naught, dear heart, this morn as ever was, on the
                              road to Zoagli,
    And I looked the other way.

How fared the would-be-not-humble dandy,
    With his long black cloak and his short trousers grey?
He fared ill, dear heart, this morn as ever was, on the
                              road to Zoagli,
    For dead he lay.

MAX BEERBOHM

The Shubble

There was an old man said, 'I fear
    That life, my dear friends, is a bubble,
Still, with all due respect to a Philistine ear,
    A limerick's best when it's double.'
    When they said, 'But the waste
      Of time, temper, taste!'
He gulped down his ink with cantankerous haste,
    And chopped off his head with a shubble.

WALTER DE LA MARE

Buttons

There was an old skinflint of Hitching
Had a cook, Mrs. Casey, of Cork;
There was nothing but crusts in the kitchen,
While in parlour was sherry and pork.
So at last, Mrs. Casey, her pangs to assuage,
Having snipped off his buttonses, curried the page;
And now, while that skinflint gulps sherry and pork
In his parlour adjacent to Hitching,
To the tune blithe and merry of knife and of fork,
Anthropophagy reigns in the kitchen.

WALTER DE LA MARE

Archery

To place one's little boy—just *so*—
An apple on his head,
Then loose an arrow from one's bow
And not to shoot him dead:—

That is a feat requiring skill,
And confidence as well;
As any archer would have told
The man who tolled the bell.

The luck must hold; the child stand still;
This William befell;
But just how close was core to corse
Could only William tell.

WALTER DE LA MARE

Green

There was an old grocer of Goring
Had a butter assistant named Green,
Who sank through a hole in the flooring
And never was afterwards seen.
  Did he look in his cellar?
  Did he miss the poor fellow?
  Not at all. Quite phlegmatic,
  He retired to an attic,
And there watched the moon in her glory o'er Goring—
  A sight not infrequently seen.

WALTER DE LA MARE

J. J.

There was an old vicar of Sinder
Had a sexton named Jeremy Jones,
He'd watch him from out of his winder—
And smile at him digging up bones;
  Then, hid in a curtain,
  To make sound uncertain,
He'd holla, 'Hello, there! OLD JONES! J. Jones!'
  And Jones, like an owl,
  Would peer o'er his showl,
And wonder from which of his old friends in Sinder
  Had burst out that muffled, 'Old Jones!'

WALTER DE LA MARE

False Dawn

My old friend, Lord O., owned a parcel of land—
A waste of wild dunes, rushes, marram and sand—
With a square Tudor mansion—not a bush, not a tree—
Looking over salt flats a full league to the sea;
    And at his demise he bequeathed it to me. . . .

It was dusk as I entered. A gull to its mates
Cackled high in the air as I passed through the gates,
And out of the distance—full twenty miles wide—
Came the resonant boom of the incoming tide:
    Gulls' scream and groundswell, and nothing beside.

In the cold of the porch I tugged at the bell,
Till the bowels of the house echoed back like a knell.
I hearkened; then peered through the hole in the lock;
And a voice, cold and clammy, inquired, 'Did you knock?'
    And there was Lord O.—in his funeral smock.

In silence he watched me, then led me upstairs
To a room where a table stood, flanked by two chairs;
For light but a dip, in an old silver stick,
With guttering grease and a long unsnuffed wick;
    And he said, 'If you're hungry, eat quick.'

So I sipped his cold water and nibbled his bread,
While he gazed softly out from the holes in his head:—
'You would hardly believe, Brown, when once I was gone,
How I craved for your company—where there is none;
    Shivered and craved—on and on.

'This house, I agree, may seem cheerless to you;
But glance from that window! By Gad, what a view!
And think, when we weary of darkness and rats,

We can share the long night with the moon and the bats,
  And wander for hours on those flats.

'And when in the East creeping daybreak shows wan,
You'll excuse me, I know, if I have to be gone,
For as soon as sounds cock-crow, the red and the grey,
It's a rule with us all—even peers must obey—
  We all have to hasten away.'

So that is my fate now. The small hours draw near,
We shall stalk arm-in-arm in that scenery drear;
Tête-à-tête by blanched breakers discuss on and on
If it's better to be flesh and blood or mere bone,
  Till it's time for Lord O. to be gone.

Yet, doubtless he means well. I would not suggest
To shun peers with property always is best.
But insomnia, nightmare, tic-douloureux, cramp,
Have reduced me to what's little short of a scamp;
For I've hung in my hen-roost a very large lamp.
And now, well, at least two full hours before day,
  Lord O., he hears cock-crow, the red and the grey;
  Sighs; stares at the ocean—and hastens away.

WALTER DE LA MARE

The Waif

There lived a small hermaphrodite beside the silver Brent,
A stream meandering not in maps of Surrey, Bucks, or Kent;
Yet jealous elves from these sweet parts, this tiny mite to vex,
Would tease, torment, and taunt, and call him, 'Master
  Middlesex!

He lived on acorns, dewdrops, cowslips, bilberries, and snow—
A small, shy, happy, tuneful thing, and innocent of woe;
Except when these malignant imps, his tenderness to vex,
Would tease, torment, and taunt, and call him, 'Master
     Middlesex!'

He ran away; he went to sea; to far Peru he came.
There where the Ataquipa flows and odorous cinchona
     blows and no one knows his name,
He nests now with the humming-bird that sips but never pecks;
And silent slides the silver Brent, and mute is 'Middlesex.'

WALTER DE LA MARE

Bishop Winterbourne

The Reverend William Winterbourne,
When walking in the Mall,
Tired of genteel pedestrians,
Much yearned to meet a *pal*,
Or, failing an old crony,
     His best gal.

Beelzebub decoyed that wish up.
The Reverend William's now a bishop.
Now, when he fares down Piccadilly,
His blameless Conscience—willy-nilly—
So archepiscopally staid is,
He never gives a thought to ladies.
Heedless of impious scrutinies
The curious fix on all D.D.'s,
His gaiters 'neath his apron wend;
His steps in one direction bend;
His heart, as right as reverend,
Has for desire one only end—

To wit, to join the wild Te Deum
That echoes through the Athenaeum.

WALTER DE LA MARE

March Hares

'The best way to go,' said my muffled-up friend, 'is to look in
  its *form* for a Hare, you know';
So, with gun over shoulder, we sallied out early, the bushes all
  hunched up with snow, you know;
The dawn was still under the eastern horizon, and O but the
  morning was rare, you know;
The elms and the oaks were a-dangle with ice, that swayed in
  the breeze to and fro, you know—
Icicles half a yard long at the least, that tinkled and rang in the
  air, you know;
'A marvellous music,' said I to my friend; and he, he never
  said, No, you know.

The snow had been falling for days, there were drifts full
  fifteen feet deep, and so fair, you know,
Aurora herself might have looked to her blushes, and Cupid
  have trimmed up his bow, you know;
And when o'er the rim of the World came the Sun, and with
  eye like a topaz did glare, you know,
We stood for a while as if blinded with Paradise, dumb in that
  wonderful glow, you know;
We coughed, and we shifted our guns, and went on—no more
  than a cough could we dare, you know.
For a moment by moment we couldn't tell where we should
  come within sight of the foe, you know.

And, all of a sudden, my friend, he said, 'Ssh!' and I looked
  and I listened; and there, you know—

Not half a shot off, with his ears and his scut, crouching close
   in the lily-white snow, you know,
And his eyes like two blazing bright marbles of glass—sat
   staring and glaring a Hare, you know!
The sun it shone brighter, the blue it grew bluer, the heavens
   like an infinite O, you know,
And a breeze out of nowhere rang sweet as a bell rings, and
   stirred in our whiskers and hair, you know.

My friend—then—he—up—with—his—gun—to—his—
   shoulder—and tugged at the trigger: but lo! you know,
In his kindness of heart he'd forgotten to load, for for
   slaughter he didn't much care, you know;
We laughed, oh! laughed we; and, my ghost! if old Watt
   didn't up with his nose and cry, 'Ho!' you know;
And stamped for his brothers and sisters to come; and they
   hopped up in scores from their lairs, you know.
They danced, they fandangoed, they scuttered, they·sang,
   turned somersaults, leapfrogged, and so, you know
We trudged back to breakfast with nothing to jug, which
   wasn't *exacaly* fair, you know,
      Which *wasn't* exacaly fair.

WALTER DE LA MARE

On the Dangers attending Altruism
on the High Seas

   Observe these Pirates bold and gay,
      that sail a gory sea:
   notice their bright expression:—
      the handsome one is me.

   We plundered ships and harbours,
      we spoiled the Spanish main;

but Nemesis watched over us,
   for it began to rain.

Oh all well-meaning folk take heed!
   Our Captain's fate was sore;
a more well-meaning Pirate,
   had never dripped with gore.

The rain was pouring long and loud,
   the sea was drear and dim;
a little fish was floating there:
   our Captain pitied him.

'How sad,' he said, and dropped a tear,
   splash on the cabin roof,
'that we are dry, while he is there
   without a waterproof.

'We'll get him up on board at once;
   for Science teaches me,
he will be wet if he remains
   much longer in the sea.'

They fished him out; the First Mate wept,
   and came with rugs and ale:
the Boatswain brought him one golosh,
   and fixed it on his tail.

But yet he never loved the ship;
   against the mast he'd lean:
if spoken to, he coughed and smiled,
   and blushed a pallid green.

Though plied with hardbake, beef and beer,
   he showed no wish to sup:
the neatest riddles they could ask,
   he always gave them up.

They seized him and court-martialled him,
   in some excess of spleen,
for lack of social sympathy,
   (Victoria XII. 18).

They gathered every evidence
   that might remove a doubt:
they wrote a postcard in his name,
   and partly scratched it out.

Till, when his guilt was clear as day,
   with all formality,
they doomed the traitor to be drowned,
   and threw him in the sea.

The flashing sunset, as he sank,
   made every scale a gem;
and, turning with a graceful bow,
   he kissed his fin to them.

Moral

I am, I think I have remarked,
   terrifically old
(the second Ice-age was a farce,
   the first was rather cold).

A friend of mine, a Trilobite,
   had gathered in his youth,
when Trilobites *were* Trilobites,
   this all-important truth.

We aged ones play solemn parts—
   sire—guardian—uncle—king.
Affection is the salt of life,
   kindness a noble thing.

The old alone may comprehend
  a sense in my decree;
but—if you find a fish on land,
  oh throw it in the sea.

G. K. CHESTERTON

The Oneness of the Philosopher
with Nature

I love to see the little Stars
  all dancing to one tune;
I think quite highly of the Sun,
  and kindly of the Moon.

The million forests of the Earth
  come trooping in to tea.
The great Niagara waterfall
  is never shy with me.

I am the Tiger's confidant,
  and never mention names:
the Lion drops the formal 'Sir,'
  and lets me call him James.

Into my ear the blushing Whale
  stammers his love. I know
why the Rhinoceros is sad,
  —ah, child! 'twas long ago.

I am akin to all the Earth
  by many a tribal sign:
the aged Pig will often wear
  that sad, sweet smile of mine.

My niece, the Barnacle, has got
  my piercing eyes of black;
the Elephant has got my nose,
  I do not want it back.

I know the strange tale of the Slug;
  the Early Sin—the Fall—
the Sleep—the Vision—and the Vow—
  the Quest—the Crown—the Call.

And I have loved the Octopus,
  since we were boys together.
I love the Vulture and the Shark:
  I even love the weather.

I love to bask in sunny fields,
  and when that hope is vain,
I go and bask in Baker Street,
  all in the pouring rain.

Come snow! where fly, by some strange law,
  hard snowballs—without noise—
through streets untenanted, except
  by good unconscious boys.

Come fog! Exultant mystery—
  where, in strange darkness rolled,
the end of my own nose becomes
  a lovely legend old.

Come snow, and hail, and thunderbolts,
  sleet, fire, and general fuss;
come to my arms, come all at once—
  oh photograph me thus!

                              G. K. CHESTERTON

The Bards

My agèd friend, Miss Wilkinson,
  Whose mother was a Lambe,
Saw Wordsworth once, and Coleridge, too,
  One morning in her p'ram'.*

Birdlike the bards stooped over her—
  Like fledgling in a nest;
And Wordsworth said, 'Thou harmless babe!'
  And Coleridge was impressed.

The pretty thing gazed up and smiled,
  And softly murmured, 'Coo!'
William was then aged sixty-four
  And Samuel sixty-two.

WALTER DE LA MARE

* This was a three-wheeled vehicle
    Of iron and of wood;
  It had a leather apron,
    But it hadn't any hood.

Miss Pheasant

There was an old man with a gun,
Who espied an old lady named Pheasant;
She sat on a seat in the sun,
And he stared, and he stared: most unpleasant!
    But at last, drawing near,
    He made it quite clear
That he had no *intention* so rude to appear,
  But was merely confused, being out with his gun,
  At espying a lady named Pheasant.

WALTER DE LA MARE

It Might be a Lump of Amber

It might be a lump of amber, ma'am,
It might be a stick of coral;
But what we have to remember, ma'am,
Is to keep our eye on the moral.

WALTER DE LA MARE

Two Old Crows

Two old crows sat on a fence rail.
Two old crows sat on a fence rail,
Thinking of effect and cause,
Of weeds and flowers,
And nature's laws.
One of them muttered, one of them stuttered,
One of them stuttered, one of them muttered.
Each of them thought far more than he uttered.
One crow asked the other crow a riddle.
One crow asked the other crow a riddle:
The muttering crow
Asked the stuttering crow,
'Why does a bee have a sword to his fiddle?
Why does a bee have a sword to his fiddle?'
'Bee-cause,' said the other crow,
'Bee-cause,
B B B B B B B B B B B B B B B B-cause.'
Just then a bee flew close to their rail:—
'Buzzzzzzzzzzzzzzzzzzzz   zzzzzzzzz   zzzzzzzzzzzzzzz
    ZZZZZZZZ.'
And those two black crows
Turned pale,
And away those crows did sail.
Why?

B B B B B B B B B B B B B B-cause.
B B B B B B B B B B B B B B-cause.
'Buzzzzzzzzzzzzzzzzzzz   zzzzzzzzz   zzzzzzzzzzzzzzz
   ZZZZZZZZ.'

VACHEL LINDSAY

The night was growing old
    As she trudged through snow and sleet;
And her nose was long and cold,
    And her shoes were full of feet.

ANON

I wish I were

I wish I were a
Elephantiaphus
And could pick off the coconuts with my nose.
But, oh! I am not,
(Alas! I cannot be)
An Elephanti-
Elephantiaphus.
But I'm a cockroach
And I'm a water-bug,
I can crawl around and hide behind the sink.

I wish I were a
Rhinoscerèeacus
And could wear an ivory toothpick in my nose.
But, oh! I am not,
(Alas! I cannot be)
A Rhinoscōri-
Rhinoscerèeacus.
But I'm a beetle
And I'm a pumpkin-bug,
I can buzz and bang my head against the wall.

271

I wish I were a
Hippopōpotamus
And could swim the Tigris and the broad Gangès.
But, oh! I am not,
(Alas! I cannot be)
A hippopōpo–
Hippopōpotamus.
But I'm a grasshopper
And I'm a katydid,
I can play the fiddle with my left hind-leg.

I wish I were a
Levilevīathan
And had seven hundred knuckles in my spine.
But, oh! I am not,
(Alas! I cannot be)
A Levi-ikey–
A Levi-ikey-mo.
But I'm a firefly
And I'm a lightning-bug,
I can light cheroots and gaspers with my tail.

ANON

Life is Butter, Life is Butter;
Melancholy flower, Melancholy flower;
Life is but a Melon, Life is but a Melon;
Cauliflower, Cauliflower.

ANON

Did you ever, ever, ever,
In your leaf, life, loaf,
See the deevel, divil, dovol,
Kiss his weef, wife, woaf?
No, I never, never, never,

In my leaf, life, loaf,
Saw the deevel, divil, dovol,
Kiss his weef, wife, woaf.

ANON

Lines Written by a Bear of
Very Little Brain

On Monday, when the sun is hot
I wonder to myself a lot:
'Now is it true, or is it not,
That what is which and which is what?'

On Tuesday, when it hails and snows,
The feeling on me grows and grows
That hardly anybody knows
If those are these or these are those.

On Wednesday, when the sky is blue,
And I have nothing else to do,
I sometimes wonder if it's true
That who is what and what is who.

On Thursday, when it starts to freeze
And hoar-frost twinkles on the trees,
How very readily one sees
That these are whose—but whose are these?

On Friday—

A. A. MILNE

My Mammy was a Wall-Eyed Goat

My Mammy was a wall-eyed goat,
My Old Man was an ass,
And I feed myself off leather boots
And dynamite and grass;
For I'm a mule, a long-eared fool
And I ain't never been to school—
    Mammeee! Ma-ha-mam-hee!
    Heee-haw! Mamaah!
    Ma-ha-mee!

ANON

I scream
You scream
We all scream
For ice-cream.

ANON

It was a cough that carried her off,
It was a coffin they carried her off in.

ANON

Bestiaire sans Prénom

l'éléphant est amoureux du millimètre

l'escargot est fier
sous son chapeau d'or
son cuir est calme
avec un rire de flore
il porte son fusil de gélatine

274

l'aigle a des gestes de vide présumé
son pis est rempli d'éclairs

le lion porte une moustache
en pur gothique flamboyant
et des souliers pâles et purgés
comme un néo-soldat
après une défaite de lune

la langouste descend du mât
échange sa canne contre une baguette
et remonte avec son bâton
le long du tronc d'arbre

la mouche avec un regard ronflant
repose son nez sur un jet d'eau

la vache prend le chemin de parchemin
qui se perd dans un livre de chair
chaque poil de ce livre
pèse une livre

le serpent saute avec picotement et picotement
antour des cuvettes d'amour
remplies de cœurs percés de flèches
le papillon empaillé
devient un papapillon empapaillé
le papapillon empapaillé
devient un grandpapapillon grandempapaillé

le rossignol frère du sphinx
arrose des estomacs des cœurs des cerveaux des tripes
c'est-à-dire des lys des roses des œillets des lilas

la puce porte son pied droit
derrière son oreille gauche
et sa main gauche

dans sa main droite
et saute sur son pied gauche
par dessus son oreille droite

HANS ARP

I am a horse

I travel in a train
that is overcrowded
in my compartment
each seat is taken by a woman
with a man sitting on her lap
the air is unbearably tropical
all the travellers have an enormous appetite
they eat without ceasing
suddenly the men
begin to whimper
and long for the maternal breast
they unbutton the women's blouses
and suck the fresh milk to their hearts' content
I alone do not suck
nor am I suckled
nobody sits on my lap
and I'm not on anyone's lap
because I am a horse
immense and upright I sit
with my hind-legs up on the train seat
and comfortably lean
on my fore-legs
I whinny a raucous neigh neigh neigh
on my breast glitter
the sex buttons of sex appeal
in neat little rows

like the glittering buttons on uniforms
oh summertime
oh wide wide world

HANS ARP
(tr. Harriet Watts)

two little arabs adult and arabesque
played on two little hobby-horse fiddles
all at once a pipe appeared
to the two little arabs adult and arabesque
a tobacco pipe on doll's feet
at such moments points fall on our points
fat like metrical apples

but the two little arabs adult and arabesque
sneezed rather than shivered
like courageous turtles who have lost their shells
sneeze rather than shiver
they sneezed with such might
that their little hobby-horse fiddles went sailing
into a far but musical land

hereupon they were enticed by a half-filled glass
   of wine
that was halfway on its way
whose endless end ended in a bald sea
which was covered with an oil cloth
the two little arabs adult and arabesque
questioned the pipe about the half-full glass of
   wine

'the wine is mine'
replied the pipe with firmness
but continued in a juicy voice
'gorblimey gorblemony gorblorangey

drink it just the same
it is part of a still-life
indeed I might well say of a deadstill still-life
that was beginning on its way
whose endless end as everyone knows ends in a
   bald sea'

the two little arabs adult and arabesque
like two omnivorous pyramids drained
this glass half filled with wine
and devoured in addition
a box of matches three pears and an apple

whereupon they felt themselves most rococo
like pompeian pumpworkers
that pump the pompadour on the gold-leafed
   pump
from their cute little rumps they let fly giant
balloonbaskets made of skin
with great wild star eyes
which were shod in parchment shoes
and topped with polished agate hats
thereupon the two little arabs adult and arabesque
lost their cool completely
bombarded the nightingale
which struck up the alarm clocks on the porcelain
hills of the still and natural lives
with newborn four-footed stones
and then they vanished
into the aromatic arabian arumperfumeral night

HANS ARP
(tr. Harriet Watts)

when it burns before the harps and freezes behind the easels
when the leather hare stands like Venice up to its knees in
    water
when the pyramids polish their glassy horse-blinkers with
    mortal soft-boiled leftovers
a wowl is the ultimate substance

when the tears are covered with unwrinkled lids
when the sirloin-tipped shoes are worn to the bone-pope
when the free-hand sketcher with bones jutting out sketches
    the stemless egg
a wowl is the ultimate substance

when the cohorts in sin harrow with the purgatorial mops
when the allahs all trill like larks
when the four-cornered buttoned-up suns roll on
    helter-skelter with a whoa and a giddy-up
a wowl is the ultimate substance

HANS ARP
(tr. Harriet Watts)

The Dying Airman

A handsome young airman lay dying,
And as on the airfield he lay,
To the mechanics who round him came sighing,
These last dying words he did say:

'Take the cylinders out of my kidneys,
The connecting-rod out of my brain,
Take the cam-shaft from out of my backbone,
And assemble the engine again.

ANON

An Anglican curate in want
Of a second-hand portable font
    Will exchange for the same
    A photo (with frame)
Of the Bishop Elect of Vermont.

RONALD KNOX

Picnic Rhyme

Lemonade
Made in the shade,
Stirred with a spade,
By an old maid.

ANON

To the Cuckoo

O Cuckoo! shall I call thee Bird,
Or but a wandering voice?
    State the alternative preferred
    With reasons for your choice.

F. H. TOWNSEND

The Song of the Jellicles

Jellicle Cats come out to-night,
Jellicle Cats come one come all:
The Jellicle Moon is shining bright—
Jellicles come to the Jellicle Ball.

Jellicle Cats are black and white,
Jellicle Cats are rather small;
Jellicle Cats are merry and bright,
And pleasant to hear when they caterwaul.
Jellicle Cats have cheerful faces,
Jellicle Cats have bright black eyes;
They like to practise their airs and graces
And wait for the Jellicle Moon to rise.

Jellicle Cats develop slowly,
Jellicle Cats are not too big;
Jellicle Cats are roly-poly,
They know how to dance a gavotte and a jig.
Until the Jellicle Moon appears
They make their toilette and take their repose:
Jellicles wash behind their ears,
Jellicles dry between their toes.

Jellicle Cats are white and black,
Jellicle Cats are of moderate size;
Jellicles jump like a jumping-jack,
Jellicle Cats have moonlit eyes.
They're quiet enough in the morning hours,
They're quiet enough in the afternoon,
Reserving their terpsichorean powers
To dance by the light of the Jellicle Moon.

Jellicle Cats are black and white,
Jellicle Cats (as I said) are small;
If it happens to be a stormy night
They will practise a caper or two in the hall.
If it happens the sun is shining bright
You would say they had nothing to do at all:
They are resting and saving themselves to be right
For the Jellicle Moon and the Jellicle Ball.

T. S. ELIOT

The Rum Tum Tugger

The Rum Tum Tugger is a Curious Cat:
If you offer him pheasant he would rather have grouse.
If you put him in a house he would much prefer a flat,
If you put him in a flat then he'd rather have a house.
If you set him on a mouse then he only wants a rat,
If you set him on a rat then he'd rather chase a mouse.
Yes the Rum Tum Tugger is a Curious Cat—
   And there isn't any call for me to shout it:
     For he will do
     As he do do
       And there's no doing anything about it!

The Rum Tum Tugger is a terrible bore:
When you let him in, then he wants to be out;
He's always on the wrong side of every door,
And as soon as he's at home, then he'd like to get about.
He likes to lie in the bureau drawer,
But he makes such a fuss if he can't get out.
Yes the Rum Tum Tugger is a Curious Cat—
   And it isn't any use for you to doubt it:
     For he will do
     As he do do
       And there's no doing anything about it!

The Rum Tum Tugger is a curious beast:
His disobliging ways are a matter of habit.
If you offer him fish then he always wants a feast;
When there isn't any fish then he won't eat rabbit.
If you offer him cream then he sniffs and sneers,
For he only likes what he finds for himself;
So you'll catch him in it right up to the ears,
If you put it away on the larder shelf.
The Rum Tum Tugger is artful and knowing,
The Rum Tum Tugger doesn't care for a cuddle;

But he'll leap on your lap in the middle of your sewing,
For there's nothing he enjoys like a horrible muddle.
Yes the Rum Tum Tugger is a Curious Cat—
  And there isn't any need for me to spout it:
    For he will do
    As he do do
      And there's no doing anything about it!

T. S. ELIOT

Chard Whitlow

(*Mr. Eliot's Sunday Evening Postscript*)

As we get older we do not get any younger.
Seasons return, and to-day I am fifty-five,
And this time last year I was fifty-four,
And this time next year I shall be sixty-two.
And I cannot say I should care (to speak for myself)
To see my time over again—if you can call it time,
Fidgeting uneasily under a draughty stair,
Or counting sleepless nights in the crowded Tube.

There are certain precautions—though none of them very
    reliable—
Against the blast from bombs, or the flying splinter,
But not against the blast from Heaven, *vento dei venti*,
The wind within a wind, unable to speak for wind;
And the frigid burnings of purgatory will not be touched
By any emollient.
                I think you will find this put,
Far better than I could ever hope to express it,
In the words of Kharma: 'It is, we believe,
Idle to hope that the simple stirrup-pump
Can extinguish hell.'

Oh, listeners,
And you especially who have switched off the wireless,
And sit in Stoke or Basingstoke, listening appreciatively to the
    silence
(Which is also the silence of hell), pray not for yourselves but
    your souls.

And pray for me also under the draughty stair.
As we get older we do not get any younger.

And pray for Kharma under the holy mountain.

HENRY REED

Limericks

1

There once was a wonderful wizard
who got a fierce pain in the gizzard
        so he drank wind and snow
        at fifty below
and farted a forty-day blizzard.

2

On the deck of a ship called the Masm
an old salt was having a spasm
        cried a lady named Chasm
        is that an orgasm?
And the old salt replied to her, Yas'm.

3

Animula vagula blandula
is it true that your origin's glandular?
        Must you twang for the Lord
        an umbilical chord
like all other impropagandula?

It's time to make love: douse the glim,
the fireflies twinkle and dim,
    the stars lean together
    like birds of a feather
and the loin lies down with the limb.

CONRAD AIKEN

Awake, My Lute!

I stood in the gloom of a spacious room
  Where I listened for hours (on and off)
To a terrible bore with a beard like a snore
  And a heavy rectangular cough,
Who discoursed on the habits of orchids and rabbits
  And how an electron behaves
And a way to cure croup with solidified soup
  In a pattern of circular waves;
Till I suddenly spied that what stood at his side
  Was a richly upholstered baboon
With paws like the puns in a poem of Donne's
  And a tail like a voyage to the Moon.
Then I whispered, 'Look out! For I very much doubt
  If your colleague is really a man.'
But the lecturer said, without turning his head,
  'Oh, that's only the Beverage plan!'
As one might have forseen, the whole sky became green
  At this most injudicious remark,
For the Flood had begun and we both had to run
  For our place in the queue to the Ark.
Then, I hardly know how (we were swimming by now),
  The sea got all covered with scum.
Made of publishers' blurbs and irregular verbs
  Of the kind which have datives in -*um*;

And the waves were so high that far up in the sky
   We saw the grand lobster, and heard
How he snorted, 'Compare the achievements of Blair
   With the grave of King Alfred the Third,
And add a brief note and if possible quote,
   And distinguish and trace and discuss
The probable course of a Methodist horse
   When it's catching a decimal bus.'
My answer was Yes. But they marked it N.S.,
   And a truffle fish grabbed at my toe,
And dragged me deep down to a bombulous town
   Where the traffic was silent and slow.
Then a voice out of heaven observed, 'Quarter past seven!'
   And I threw all the waves off my head,
For the voice beyond doubt was the voice of my scout,
   And the bed of that sea was my bed.

C. S. LEWIS

La Sardine

Une sardine de Royan
Nageait dans l'eau de la Gironde.
Le ciel est grand, la terre est ronde,
J'irai me baigner à Royan.
Avec la sardine,
Avec la Gironde,
Vive la marine!
Et salut au monde!

ROBERT DESNOS

La Colombe de l'Arche

Maudit
soit le père de l'épouse
du forgeron qui forgea le fer de la cognée
avec laquelle le bûcheron abattit le chêne
dans lequel on sculpta le lit
où fut engendré l'arrière-grand-père
de l'homme qui conduisit la voiture
dans laquelle ta mère
rencontra ton père!

ROBERT DESNOS

Le Pélican

Le capitaine Jonathan,
Etant âgé de dix-huit ans,
Capture un jour un pélican
Dans une île d'Extrême-Orient.

Le pélican de Jonathan,
Au matin, pond un œuf tout blanc
Et il en sort un pélican
Lui ressemblant étonnamment.

Et ce deuxième pélican
Pond, à son tour, un œuf tout blanc
D'où sort, inévitablement
Un autre qui en fait autant.

Cela peut durer pendant très longtemps
Si l'on ne fait pas d'omelette avant.

ROBERT DESNOS

287

Le Géranium

Dans un pot un géranium,
Un poisson dans l'aquarium,
Géranium et poisson rouge,
Si tu bouges, si tu bouges,
Tu n'auras pas de rhum,
Géranium, géranium,
Géranium et poisson rouge.

ROBERT DESNOS

Le Lama

Lama, fils de lama
Et père de lama,
Cousin de l'alpaca,
Frère de la vigogne,
Frère du guanaco,
A pour toute besogne
D'écouter les échos
Et fuir le loup-garou
Qui vit sous son climat:
Il habite au Pérou
Capitale Lima.

ROBERT DESNOS

Les Hiboux

Ce sont les mères des hiboux
Qui désiraient chercher les poux
De leurs enfants, leurs petits choux,
En les tenant sur les genoux.

Leurs yeux d'or valent des bijoux
Leur bec est dur comme cailloux,
Ils sont doux comme des joujoux,
Mais aux hiboux point de genoux !

Votre histoire se passait où?
Chez les Zoulous? Les Andalous?
Ou dans la cabane bambou?
A Moscou? Ou à Tombouctou?
En Anjou ou dans le Poitou?
Au Pérou ou chez les Mandchous?

Hou ! Hou !
Pas du tout, c'était chez les fous.

ROBERT DESNOS

Le Kangourou

Kangourou premier, roi des kangourous,
Ayant accroché son grand sabre au clou
S'assoit dans un trône en feuilles de chou.
Sa femme arrivant, pleine de courroux,
Dans sa poche a mis ses fils et ses sous,
Ses gants, son mouchoir et ses roudoudous.

Kangourou dernier, roi des kangourous,
Avait les yeux verts et les cheveux roux.
Sa femme peignait son royal époux.
Kangourou le roux, roi des kangourous,
Kangourou dernier, kangourou le roux.

ROBERT DESNOS

Tenuous and Precarious

Tenuous and Precarious
Were my guardians,
Precarious and Tenuous,
Two Romans.

My father was Hazardous,
Hazardous,
Dear old man,
Three Romans.

There was my brother Spurious,
Spurious Posthumous,
Spurious was spurious
Was four Romans.

My husband was Perfidious,
He was perfidious,
Five Romans.

Surreptitious, our son,
Was surreptitious,
He was six Romans.

Our cat Tedious
Still lives,
Count not Tedious
Yet.

My name is Finis,
Finis, Finis,
I am Finis,
Six, five, four, three two,
One Roman,
Finis.

STEVIE SMITH

The River God

I may be smelly and I may be old,
Rough in my pebbles, reedy in my pools,
But where my fish float by I bless their swimming
And I like the people to bathe in me, especially women.
But I can drown the fools
Who bathe too close to the weir, contrary to rules.
And they take a long time drowning
As I throw them up now and then in a spirit of clowning.
Hi yih, yippity-yap, merrily I flow,
O I may be an old foul river but I have plenty of go.
Once there was a lady who was too bold
She bathed in me by the tall black cliff where the water runs
   cold,
So I brought her down here
To be my beautiful dear.
Oh will she stay with me will she stay
This beautiful lady, or will she go away?
She lies in my beautiful deep river bed with many a weed
To hold her, and many a waving reed.
Oh who would guess what a beautiful white face lies there
Waiting for me to smooth and wash away the fear
She looks at me with. Hi yih, do not let her
Go. There is no one on earth who does not forget her
Now. They say I am a foolish old smelly river
But they do not know of my wide original bed
Where the lady waits, with her golden sleepy head.
If she wishes to go I will not forgive her.

STEVIE SMITH

The Occasional Yarrow

It was a mile of greenest grass
Whereon a little stream did pass,
   The Occasional Yarrow

Only in every seventh year
Did this pretty stream appear,
  The Occasional Yarrow

Wading and warbling in its beds
Of grass decked out with daisy heads,
  The Occasional Yarrow

There in my seventh year, and this sweet stream's,
I wandered happily (as happy gleams
  The Occasional Yarrow).

Though now to memory alone
I can call up thy lovely form,
  Occasional Yarrow

I still do bless thy Seventh days
Bless thy sweet name and all who praise
  The Occasional Yarrow.

STEVIE SMITH

The Common Cormorant

The common cormorant (or shag)
Lays eggs inside a paper bag,
You follow the idea, no doubt?
It's to keep the lightning out.

But what these unobservant birds
Have never thought of, is that herds
Of wandering bears might come with buns
And steal the bags to hold the crumbs.

CHRISTOPHER ISHERWOOD

The Bereaved Swan

Wan
Swan
On the lake
Like a cake
Of soap
Why is the swan
Wan
On the lake?
He has abandoned hope.

Wan
Swan
On the lake afloat
Bows his head:
O would that I were dead
For her sake that lies
Wrapped from my eyes
In a mantle of death,
The swan saith.

STEVIE SMITH

Les ponts s'effondrent tous
au cri du paon qui pond
et les pans de ponts
transforment les rivières.

Aux lacs des lacs
meurent les paons
enlisés dans la gomme laque.

ROBERT DESNOS

293

Isabelle et Marie

Isabelle rencontra Marie au bas de l'escalier:
'Tu n'es qu'une chevelure! lui dit-elle.
—et toi une main.
—main toi-même, omoplate!
—omoplate? c'est trop fort, espèce de sein!
—langue! dent! pubis!
—œil!
—cils! aisselle! rein!
—gorge!... oreille!
—oreille? moi? regarde-toi, narine!
—non mais, vieille gencive!
—doigt!
—con!'

ROBERT DESNOS

Lord Barrenstock

Lord Barrenstock and Epicene,
What's it to me that you have been
In your pursuit of interdicted joys
Seducer of a hundred little boys?

Your sins are red about your head
And many people wish you dead.

You trod the widow in the mire
Wronged the son, deceived the sire.

You put a fence about the land
And made the people's cattle graze on sand.

Ratted from many a pool and forced amalgamation
And dealt in shares which never had a stock exchange
    quotation.

Non flocci facio, I do not care
For wrongs you made the other fellow bear:
'Tis not for these unsocial acts not these
I wet my pen. I would not have you tease,
With a repentance smug and overdue
For all the things you still desire to do,
The ears of an outraged divinity:
But oh your tie is crooked and I see
Too plain you had an éclair for your tea.

It is this nonchalance about your person—
That is the root of my profound aversion.

STEVIE SMITH

The Celtic Fringe

Kathleen ni Houlihan
Walking down the boule-igan
Ran into a hooligan
Ah ha, Kathleen ni Houlihan.

She went with the rat-ican
And very soon they had a brat-ican
Ah ha, Kathleen ni Houlihan
How goes it now?

They called him Rebel-can
Oh he was a devil-can
Kathleen ni Houlihan
Your son.

And the big black cat-ican
That sat on the mat-ican
With a pit and a pati–can
Spit. Spat.

Was the chief sport
Of the Houlihan sort
And chiefly did Rebel-can
Twitch his tail, the devil-can.

All up the boule-igan
Runs Kathleen ni Houlihan
For flirting his tail the cat is gone,
They are alone.

And that is how the Houlihan
Fell out in the boule-igan
Whose tail shall they twitch now?
Eh, Kathleen, the cat is gone.

STEVIE SMITH

A Sonnet

An amazing thing happened to me: I suddenly forgot which came first, 7 or 8.

I went to my neighbours and asked them what they thought about that.

I was really amazed when they told me that they too couldn't remember the counting sequence. They remembered 1, 2, 3, 4, 5, and 6, but they forgot what came after that.

We all went in to the grocery store at the corner of Znamensky and Basseynaya streets and asked the cashier. The cashier smiled sadly, took a tiny little hammer out of her mouth, and slightly twitching her nose, said, 'I think 7 comes after 8 in those cases where 8 comes after 7.'

We thanked the cashier and ran joyfully out of the store. But then, thinking over the cashier's words, we again fell silent, because her words turned out to make no sense.

What were we to do? We went into the summer park and counted trees. But after we reached 6, we stopped and argued.

Some thought 7 came next, and others thought that 8 came next.

We argued for a long time, but fortunately a little boy fell off a park bench and broke both jaws. This distracted us from our argument.

Then we all went home.

DANIIL KHARMS
(tr. George Gibian)

Vindication

I don't want to boast. But when Volodya hit me in the ear and spat in my eyes, I let him have it in a way he will never forget. It was then that I beat him with the little gas stove; yesterday I beat him with the flatiron. So he did not die right away. And where is there any proof that I cut off his leg that day? He was still alive. And I beat Andryusha to death only because I was carried away by my momentum. I am not at all responsible for that. Why did Andryusha and Liza Antonovna come in there? Who was forcing them to come in that door?

I've been accused of being bloodthirsty. It's been said I drank the blood. That is a lie. I only lapped up the puddles and the spots. It's natural to want to wipe out the traces of even the most innocent transgression. And I did not rape Liza Antonovna. First of all, she wasn't a virgin any more.

Secondly I was dealing with a corpse. So the accusation is beside the point. So what if she was about to have a baby! I took the child out of her. And if it wasn't capable of living, that's not my fault. I did not tear off its head. It's the fault of that thin neck. It was simply unfit for life. It's true I stomped on the dog. But it's simply cynical to accuse me of murdering a dog, when right alongside it three human lives had been lost. I'm not counting the baby. Let us say, and I might even agree, that there was a certain amount of cruelty on my part. But to try me because I defecated on those victims is, if you pardon me, absurd. Defecating is a natural human need. So how can it be something indecent?

297

I do understand certain fears my defense attorney has, but I believe I shall be completely vindicated.

DANIIL KHARMS
(tr. George Gibian)

The Connection

Philosopher!

1. I am writing to you in answer to your letter which you are about to write to me in answer to my letter which I wrote to you.

2. A violinist bought a magnet and was carrying it home. Along the way, hoodlums jumped on him and knocked his cap off his head. The wind picked up the cap and carried it down the street.

3. The violinist put the magnet down and ran after the cap. The cap fell in a puddle of nitric acid and dissolved.

4. In the meantime, the hoodlums picked up the magnet and hid.

5. The violinist returned home without a coat and without a cap because the cap had dissolved in the nitric acid, and the violinist, upset by losing his cap, had left his coat in the streetcar.

6. The conductor of the streetcar took the coat to a second-hand shop and exchanged it there for sour cream, groats, and tomatoes.

7. The conductor's father-in-law ate too many tomatoes, became sick, and died. The corpse of the conductor's father-in-law was put in the morgue, but it got mixed up, and in place of the conductor's father-in-law, they buried some old woman.

8. On the grave of the old woman, they put a white post with the inscription 'Anton Sergeevich Kondratev.'

9. Eleven years later the worms had eaten through the post and it fell down. The cemetery watchman sawed the post in four pieces and burned it in his stove. The wife of the cemetery watchman cooked cauliflower soup over that fire.

10. But when the soup was ready, a fly fell from the wall directly into the pot with this soup. They gave the soup to the beggar Timofey.

11. The beggar Timofey ate the soup and told the beggar Nikolay that the cemetery watchman was a good-natured man.

12. The next day the beggar Nikolay went to the cemetery watchman and asked for money. But the cemetery watchman gave nothing to the beggar Nikolay and chased him away.

13. The beggar Nikolay became very angry and set fire to the cemetery watchman's house.

14. The fire spread from the house to the church, and the church burned down.

15. A long investigation was carried on but did not succeed in determining the cause of the fire.

16. In the place where the church had stood a club was built, and on the day the club opened a concert was organized, at which the violinist who fourteen years earlier had lost his coat, performed.

17. In the audience sat the son of one of those hoodlums who fourteen years before had knocked the cap off that violinist.

18. After the concert was over they rode home in the same streetcar. In the streetcar behind theirs, the driver was the same conductor who once upon a time had sold the violinist's coat in a secondhand shop.

19. And so here they are, riding late at night through the city; in front the violinist and the hoodlum's son; and in the back, the driver, the former conductor.

20. They ride along and don't know what connection there is between them, and they won't know till the day they die.

DANIIL KHARMS
(tr. George Gibian)

[The Witch's Work Song]

Two spoons of sherry
Three oz. of yeast,
Half a pound of unicorn,
And God bless the feast.
Shake them in the collander,
Bang them to a chop,
Simmer slightly, snip up nicely,
Jump, skip, hop.
Knit one, knot one, purl two together,
Pip one and pop one and pluck the secret feather.

Baste in a mod. oven.
God bless our coven.
Tra-la-la!
Three toads in a jar.
Te-he-he!
Put in the frog's knee.
Peep out of the lace curtain.
There goes the Toplady girl, she's up to no good
    that's certain.
Oh, what a lovely baby!
How nice it would go with gravy.
Pinch the salt,
Turn the malt
With a hey-nonny-nonny and I don't mean maybe.

T. H. WHITE

My Cats

I like to toss him up and down
A heavy cat weighs half a Crown
With a hey do diddle my cat Brown.

300

I like to pinch him on the sly
When nobody is passing by
With a hey do diddle my cat Fry.

I like to ruffle up his pride
And watch him skip and turn aside
With a hey do diddle my cat Hyde.

Hey Brown and Fry and Hyde my cats
That sit on tombstone for your mats.

STEVIE SMITH

Correspondence between Mr. Harrison in Newcastle and Mr. Sholto Peach Harrison in Hull

Sholto Peach Harrison you are no son of mine
And do you think I bred you up to cross the River Tyne
And do you think I bred you up (and mother says the same)
And do you think I bred you up to live a life of shame
To live a life of shame my boy as you are thinking to
Down south in Kingston-upon Hull a traveller in glue?
Come back my bonny boy nor break your father's heart
Come back and marry Lady Susan Smart
She has a mint in Anglo-Persian oil
And Sholto never more need think of toil.

You are an old and evil man my father
I tell you frankly Sholto had much rather
Travel in glue unrecompensed unwed
Than go to church with oily Sue and afterwards to bed.

STEVIE SMITH

301

From *Mots d'Heures: Gousses, Rames*
(Mother Goose Rhymes)

I

Un petit d'un petit[1]
S'étonne aux Halles[2]
Un petit d'un petit
Ah! degrés te fallent[3]
Indolent qui ne sort cesse[4]
Indolent qui ne se mène[5]
Qu'importe un petit d'un petit
Tout Gai de Reguennes.[6]

[1] The inevitable result of a child marriage.

[2] The subject of this epigrammatic poem is obviously from the provinces, since a native Parisian would take this famous old market for granted.

[3] Since this personage bears no titles, we are led to believe that the poet writes of one of those unfortunate idiot-children that in olden days existed as a living skeleton in their family's closet. I am inclined to believe, however, that this is a fine piece of misdirection and that the poet is actually writing of some famous political prisoner, or the illegitimate offspring of some noble house. The Man in the Iron Mask, perhaps?

[4], [5] Another misdirection. Obviously it was not laziness that prevented this person's going out and taking himself places.

[6] He was obviously prevented from fulfilling his destiny, since he is compared to Gai de Reguennes. This was a young squire (to one of his uncles, a Gaillard of Normandy) who died at the tender age of twelve of a surfeit of Saracen arrows before the walls of Acre in 1191.

2

Oh, les mots d'heureux bardes
Où en toutes heures que partent.[1]
Tous guetteurs pour dock à Beaune.[2]
Besoin gigot d'air.
De que paroisse paire.[3]
Et ne pour dock, pet-de-nonne.[4]

[1] Minstrels were no doubt a happy lot, and it is not surprising that

France, a cradle of wit and culture, could turn them out in such numbers that they came and went on an almost predictable schedule. As one came in the portcullis, another left by the oubliette.

[2] Beaune. Town in the Côte-d'Or, 11,000 pop., famed for its wines and mustard. It is not a port, therefore, why should everyone watch its docks? Certainly it does not have any particular renown as a center of contraband.

[3] This must refer to the Côte-d'Or, a peerless parish indeed. Rich in some of the finest vintages of France and, if we are to believe the previous line, a great lambing country.

[4] Pet-de-nonne. An extremely light and fluffy pastry. Although any decent French housewife would ask for them without hesitation at her favorite pâtisserie, delicacy forbids a direct translation here.

3

Et qui rit des curés d'Oc?[1]
De Meuse raines,[2] houp! de cloques.[3]
De quelles loques ce turque coin.[4]
Et ne d'ânes ni rennes,
Écuries des curés d'Oc.[5]

[1] Oc (or Languedoc), ancient region of France, with its capita at Toulouse. Its monks and curates were, it seems, a singularly humble and holy group. This little poem is a graceful tribute to their virtues.

[2] Meuse, or Maas, River, 560 miles long, traversing France, Belgium, and the Netherlands; Raines, old French word for frogs (from the L., *ranae*). Here is a beautiful example of Gothic imagery: He who laughs at the curés of Oc will have frogs leap at him from the Meuse river and

[3] infect him with a scrofulous disease! This is particularly interesting when we consider the widespread superstition in America that frogs and toads cause warts.

[4] 'Turkish corners' were introduced into Western Europe by returning Crusaders, among other luxuries and refinements of Oriental living. Our good monks made a concession to the fashion, but N.B. their Turkish corner was made of rags! This affectation of interior decorating had a widespread revival in the U.S.A. at the turn of the century. Ah, the Tsar's bazaars' bizarre beaux-arts.

[5] So strict were the monks that they didn't even indulge themselves in their arduous travels. No fancy mules nor reindeer in *their* stables. They iust rode around on their plain French asses.

303

4

Amboise élite gueule, chic à d'élite écoeure-le
Ratine d'émis de l'eau va fort raide.
Oing chinoise goutte, chinoise béribéri goutte
Beau doucane chinoise batte, j'y vais aux rides.[1]

---

[1] The poet reveals his feelings quite clearly anent the élite. He finds their elegance disgusting and their red clothing with a high nap stiff and uncomfortable. Their taste for Oriental ointments, fancied exotic maladies and childish attempts to smuggle their purchases makes him grow old before his time. The high moral tone of these fragments precludes the assumption that it might be just envy.

Compare Horace's *'Persicos odi, puer, apparatus . . .'*

5

L'ile déjà accornée . . .[1]
Satinées cornées . . .[2]
Y diner guérisse masse bâille . . .[3]
Il se taquine costumes[4]
Et ne poule d'août des plumes[5]
Et ne ses doigts des gouttes beaux émaille.[6]

---

[1] The (lord of the) island already has horns. This would seem to be a rehash of the old Tristram and Iseult legend; however, it is so fragmentary that positive identification is impossible.

[2] 'Satiny corneas' for 'velvet eyes,' obviously a partial description of the lady in the case.

[3] Yawns help digest a heavy dinner: a thumbnail sketch of the dull, lethargic husband.

[4] He was teased about his clothes. He was not only dull, but sloppy and inelegant.

[5] He looked like a moulting chicken in August.

[6] She wore nail polish! An interesting revelation of the antiquity of cosmetics. The Egyptians used enamel-like paints; the Chinese, jeweled guards. The timeless universality of nail decoration, alas, gives us no clue as to the possible date of these verses.

6

Raia[1] qu'écorce turban béret crosse[2]
Toussez afin laide y appeau[3] nez ouate torse.[4]
Rhinanthes heure fine guerre,[5] sans bel sonneur tôt.[6]
Chiches.[7] Lave moujik ou est révère chicot.[8]

[1] Name given to non-Mohammedan Turks.

[2] We must assume that this fragment describes a Turkish convert who forsook the turban for the biretta and crozier of a bishop and whose greatest fame was as a missionary.

[3] *Appeau.* A whistle used a as bird lure. Although his voice was ugly and he suffered from a bad cough, he must have achieved some fame as a preacher.

[4] This would indicate a singularly homely man with a stuffed nose as big as his body. Poetic license permits a certain amount of exaggeration, after all.

[5] *Rhinanthes.* A common European weed, sometimes called a 'cock's-comb.' This is a very obscure phrase and must refer to some incident during or just after a war. Perhaps this weed overran a battlefield somewhat like the poppies of Flanders after World War I.

[6] There is no doubt that this refers to some primitive mission church which had no bells.

[7] *Chiches.* Chick-peas, the staple item of diet among primitive peoples and missionary monks, known in Europe from earliest historical times.

[8] This man apparently converted and baptized an obscure Russian tribe given to worshipping tree stumps. A curious survival of Druidic religion.

7

Pas de caique, pas de caique,[1] bécasse,[2] mâne,[3]
Bec ami est coquille[4] à ce vaste Assise ou Cannes[5]
Roulette[6] et n'épate[7] éden[8] marcou[9] y débit.[10]
Ainé petit inédit, oh, vaine![11] fort bébé ennemi.[12]

[1] *Caïque.* A long narrow boat commonly used in the Levant.
[2] A shore bird, the snipe.
[3] *Mâne.* In Roman mythology, the soul after death, i.e., a ghost.
[4] 'The beak is friendly to shells.' Birds have been the subject of many

poems, and here tribute is paid to a ghostly snipe which does its own wading and swimming and feeds on shellfish.

[5] Its range is from Cannes on the Riviera to Assisi in Italy, shrine of St. Francis, patron of birds.

[6] A gambling game made famous by the Casinos of Monte Carlo and the Riviera.

[7, 8] Comment that such an attraction (roulette) is unnecessary in this astonishing earthly paradise.

[9] This refers to a man with a magic symbol on his body who is believed to have supernatural powers, but note that

[10] even he suffers losses.

[11] From the eldest to the yet unborn—All is Vanity.

[12] I don't know what child psychologists would have to say on this subject, but this bears out a suspicion I have long harbored. Babies hate people! It would be interesting to know at what age this hatred turns to dependence and affection, or whether it persists in the subconscious, subject to reawakening by the pressures and tensions of our age.

8

Reine, reine, gueux éveille.
Gomme à gaine, en horreur, taie.[1]

[1] 'Queen, Queen, arouse the rabble
Who use their girdles, horrors, as pillow slips.'

LUIS D'ANTIN VAN ROOTEN

Egocentric

What care I if good God be
If he be not good to me,
If he will not hear my cry
Nor heed my melancholy midnight sigh?
What care I if he created Lamb,
And golden Lion, and mud-delighting Clam,
And Tiger stepping out on padded toe,
And the fecund earth the Blindworms know?

He made the Sun, the Moon and every Star,
He made the infant Owl and the Baboon,
He made the ruby-orbed Pelican,
He made all silent inhumanity,
Nescient and quiescent to his will,
Unquickened by the questing conscious flame
That is my glory and my bitter bane.
What care I if Skies are blue,
If God created Gnat and Gnu,
What care I if good God be
If he be not good to me?

STEVIE SMITH

Our Bog is Dood

Our Bog is dood, our Bog is dood,
They lisped in accents mild,
But when I asked them to explain
They grew a little wild.
How do you know your Bog is dood
My darling little child?

We know because we wish it so
That is enough, they cried,
And straight within each infant eye
Stood up the flame of pride,
And if you do not think it so
You shall be crucified.

Then tell me, darling little ones,
What's dood, suppose Bog is?
Just what we think, the answer came,
Just what we think it is.
They bowed their heads. Our Bog is ours
And we are wholly his.

But when they raised them up again
They had forgotten me
Each one upon each other glared
In pride and misery
For what was dood, and what their Bog
They never could agree.

Oh sweet it was to leave them then,
And sweeter not to see,
And sweetest of all to walk alone
Beside the encroaching sea,
The sea that soon should drown them all,
That never yet drowned me.

STEVIE SMITH

Everything is Swimming

Everything is swimming in a wonderful wisdom
She said everything was swimming in a wonderful wisdom
Silly ass
What a silly woman
Perhaps she is drunk
No I think it is mescalin
Silly woman
What a silly woman
Yes perhaps it is mescalin
It must be something
Her father, they say ...
And that funny man William ...
Silly ass
What a silly woman

Elle continua de rire comme une hyène.

STEVIE SMITH

Acknowledgements

The following are thanked for their permission to include copyright poems:

The estate of the late Conrad Aiken for limericks from *A Seizure of Limericks* (W. H. Allen).

Harriet Watts for three translations of poems by Hans Arp, 'I am a horse', 'two little Arabs adult and arabesque' and 'when it burns before the harps', from *Three Painter Poets*, tr. Harriet Watts.

William Heinemann Ltd. and The Stephen Greene Press for two poems by the late Sir Max Beerbohm, from *Max in Verse: Rhymes and Parodies*, collected and ed. J. G. Riewald. Copyright © 1963 by J. G. Riewald.

A. D. Peters & Co. Ltd. for two poems from Hilaire Belloc's *Sonnets and Verse* (Duckworth), and Gerald Duckworth & Co. Ltd. for nine poems from his *Cautionary Verses*.

A. P. Watt Ltd. for a limerick by Arnold Bennett.

Simpkin Marshall for nine poems by Gelett Burgess from *The Burgess Nonsense Book* (1914).

Miss Dorothy Collins, literary executrix of G. K. Chesterton, for two poems by G. K. Chesterton from his *Greybeards at Play* (new edition, Elek Books Ltd., 1974).

Librairie Gründ, Paris, for six poems from *Chantefables et Chantefleurs* by Robert Desnos.

Éditions Gallimard, Paris, for three poems from *Corps et biens* by Robert Desnos.

The Literary Trustees of Walter de la Mare and the Society of Authors as their representatives for twelve poems from *The Complete Poems of Walter de la Mare* (Faber).

Faber & Faber Ltd. for two poems from T. S. Eliot's *Old Possum's Book of Practical Cats*.

The Society of Authors as the literary representatives of the Estate of A. E. Housman, and Jonathan Cape Ltd., publishers of A. E. Housman's *Collected Poems*, for six poems from *A.E.H.*, ed. Laurence Housman (Cape), and for 'Fragment of a Greek Tragedy'.

Christopher Isherwood for his poem 'The Common Cormorant'.

Cornell University Press for three translations of Daniil Kharms in *Russia's Lost Literature of the Absurd*, tr. and ed. George Gibian.

The National Trust and Eyre Methuen Ltd. for a poem, 'The Under-taker's Horse', from *The Definitive Edition of Rudyard Kipling's Verse*.

A. P. Watt Ltd. for a limerick by Ronald Knox from his *In Three Tongues*.

The Literary Estate of C. S. Lewis for 'Awake, my Lute!'

Macmillan Publishing Co. Inc., U.S.A., for a poem from Vachel Lindsay's *Collected Poems* (Macmillan), copyright 1917 by Macmillan, renewed 1945 by Elizabeth C. Lindsay.

Methuen Children's Books Ltd. for a poem from A. A. Milne's *Winnie-the-Pooh*.

Routledge & Kegan Paul Ltd. for R. F. C. Hull's translation of Morgenstern's 'The Knee on its Own' in their translation of Huizinga's *Homo Ludens*, and Beacon Press, U.S.A., for Canadian rights.

Jonathan Cape Ltd. for a poem from Henry Reed's *A Map of Verona*.

James MacGibbon, literary executor of Stevie Smith, for eleven poems from *The Collected Poems of Stevie Smith* (Allen Lane).

Angus & Robertson (UK) Ltd. for eight pieces from the late L. d'A. Van Rooten's *Mots d'Heures: Gousses Rames*, and Viking Press Inc., U.S.A., for the Canadian rights.

William Collins & Co. Ltd. for 'The Witch's Work Song' from the late T. H. White's *The Sword in the Stone*.

While every effort has been made to secure permission, it has in a few cases proved impossible to trace the author or his executor. We apologize for our apparent negligence.

Sources and Notes

Titles between square brackets have been supplied by the editor.

17 MANNERLY MARGERY. *pode:* toad. *fode:* con-man. *hackney:* woman for hire, tart. *frumple:* tumble. *japed:* tricked.

18 MY LADY WENT TO CANTERBURY. *Christmas carolles newly imprinted* c. 1550. *boot:* aid. *make a mow:* make a face. *brent:* burnt. *laverock:* lark.

19 SHROVETIDE'S COUNTENANCE. Rabelais, *Pantagruel*, chap. XXXII of Book IV, translated by Peter Motteux, 1708. Rabelais's Fourth Book was published in French in 1548. Xenomanes continues his description to Pantagruel of the 'meagre-looked, lozelly', wicked prince Shrovetide (Quaresmeprenant in the French). *grigs:* small eels. *slabbered:* dribbled. *spatterdashes:* leather leggings. *funked:* farted.

20 I WILL HAVE THE WHETSTONE. R. L. Greene, *Early English Carols*, 1935. *have the whetstone:* to be awarded the whetstone (for sharpening one's tongue) was to be given the prize for tall stories. *seething souse:* boiling pig-meat. *urchin:* hedgehog. *shape:* cut out (cloth). *burdens bind:* tie up loads. *clewens:* balls of yarn. *kyrchers:* kerchiefs. *plash:* lay.

22 THE WHITE DOVE. W. Wager's morality play *The longer thou livest, the more foole thou art*, 1569.

22 A TETRASTICH. *Pantagruel*, chap. XLVII, Book III, 1546.

22 THE THREE WISE MEN OF GOTHAM. Halliwell, *The Nursery Rhymes of England*, 1853, with the substitution of the first stanza from the broadside ballad of 1632 (see I. and P. Opie, *Oxford Dictionary of Nursery Rhymes*), thus restoring the poem to the Men of Gotham, the noodle village (in the Midlands, s.w. of Nottingham) of English tradition. The nonsensical activities of the Gothamites were celebrated as early as the fifteenth century, and no doubt earlier still. But then making fun of the Welsh became an Elizabethan and Jacobean game, so the Gothamites escaped for a while. That broadside ballad of 1632 tries to have it both

ways: the Gothamites are English noodles out hunting, but they are doing it on St. David's Day as if they were Welshmen.

26 MOCKADO, FUSTIAN, AND MOTLEY. John Taylor, *Odcombs Complaint*, 1613. *maw:* a card game.

27 HA HA! HA HA! THIS WORLD DOTH PASS. Thomas Weelkes, *Airs*, 1608.

27 MARTIN SAID TO HIS MAN. Edward Ravenscroft, *Deuteromelia*, 1609. *clouting:* hobnailing.

29 UT, RE, MI, FA, SOL, LA. Edward Ravenscroft, *Pammelia*, 1609. *boot:* help. Ut, re, mi, etc.: notes of the gamut.

30 UT, RE, MI, FA, MI, RE, UT. ibid. A nonsense mixture of fun and religion—the old religion. *Quando coeli* recalling the Burial Service according to the Use of Sarum, *Libera me, Domine, de morte aeterna in die illa tremenda. Quando coeli movendi sunt et terra, dum veneris iudicare saeculum per ignem*—Deliver me, O Lord, from everlasting death in that dreadful day, when heaven and earth shall quake, when thou shalt come to judge the world by fire.

30 A NON SEQUITOR. *slipshoed:* slippered. *crock:* turn black. *threed:* thread. *mulsack:* mulled sack. *meal-mouthed:* mealy-mouthed, soft spoken. *powl:* poll, clip. *lowbell:* a bell used in wildfowling. *ganne:* bark like a fox.

31 NONSENSE. *slipshoo:* slipper. *fizzle:* noiseless fart. *humbles:* entrails.

32 A COPY OF NON SEQUITORS. Portland MSS. PW v. 37, University Library, Nottingham. *Jack of Lent:* male Aunt Sally, set up in Lent and pelted.

32 IF ALL THE WORLD WERE PAPER. Bodleian MSS. Ashmole 36. *Witts' Recreations*, 1641.

33 THE MAN IN THE WILDERNESS. Northall, *English Folk-Rhymes*, 1892.

Probably seventeenth century. cf. in Richard Brome's comedy *The Antipodes*, 1640

> But sure his mind
> Is in a wilderness: For there he sayes
> Are Geese that have two heads a peece.

34 NONSENSE. *Wit and Drollery*, 1656. *woodknife:* huntsman's short sword or dagger. *Geneva print:* either pages of a Geneva Bible or pleated linen as worn by Puritan wives. *carbonado'd:* grilled. *white-pots:* cream or custard pudding.

35 A FANCY. *Wits Merriment: or, Lusty Drollery*, 1656.

35 THREE BLIND MICE. *Catch that Catch Can*, 1658.

35 AD JOHANNUELEM LEPOREM. *Wits Restor'd*, 1658.

37 WHEN A TWISTER, A-TWISTING. John Wallis, *Grammatica Linguae Anglicanae*, 1653.

37 from THE VISION OF MAC CONGLINNE, Kuno Meyer, *Ancient Irish Poetry*, 1911.

40 AN INVITATION TO LUBBERLAND. In this version from a broadside c. 1686. For earlier and later versions see the *Faber Book of Popular Verse*, ed. Geoffrey Grigson, 1971 (Nos. 226 and 228, with note).

43 PETER PIPER. J. O. Halliwell, *Nursery Rhymes of England*, 1853.

43 BRIAN O'LINN. B. J. O'Donoghue, *The Humour of Ireland* n.d. There are many versions, English, Irish and Scottish, with the hero variously named Brian, Tommy and Tam. A form of the final stanza is quoted in W. Wager's *The longer thou livest, the more foole thou art*, 1569.

44 WHEN GOOD KING ARTHUR RULED THIS LAND. J. O. Halliwell, *Nursery Rhymes of England*, 1853.

45 THE DERBY RAM. Alfred Williams, *Folk-songs of the Upper Thames*, 1923.

47 THE RED HERRING. Versions are known in most parts of England and in America, and it is still popular like *The Derby Ram*. Folklorists make rather a meal of it—'a list of magic effects that once had to do with the creation of the cosmos', and so on—a serious 'once' which must have been a very long time ago.

49 THERE WAS A MAN OF THESSALY. *Tom Thumb's Pretty Song Book*, c. 1744. But earlier no doubt.

49 THE DIVINE BLACKSMITH. From Matthew Prior's *The Hind and the Panther Transvers'd*, 1687.

49 IL ÉTAIT UN PETIT HOMME. Claude Roy, *Trésor de la Poésie populaire*, 1954.

52 NAMBY-PAMBY. Nonsense ridicule of the sometimes childish verse of Ambrose Philips (1675?–1749). *Mammy Andromache:* Philips adapted Racine's *Andromaque* as *The Distressed Mother*.

55 MONSIEUR DE LA PALISSE. Claude Roy, *Trésor de la Poésie populaire*, 1954. This famous run of *lapalissades*, or nonsense examples of the obvious, comically perverted a rhyme—or so it was said—about the death of a sixteenth-century Marshal of France, Jacques de Chabannes, Seigneur de la Palice.

59 THE GRAND PANJANDRUM. Printed (without a mention of Samuel Foote) by Maria Edgeworth in her *Harry and Lucy Concluded*, 1825. Foote the wit and dramatist is said to have made it up to tease the actor Charles Macklin, at one of Macklin's lecture entertainments in 1755, Macklin having boasted that he had only to hear something once to be able to repeat it. One can feel sure that *The Grand Panjandrum* was known to Edward Lear, no doubt from its reappearance in an article on Foote in the *Quarterly Review* in 1854 (XCV, 516).

65 WE'RE ALL IN THE DUMPS. *Blackwood's Edinburgh Magazine*, July 1824 (according to the *Oxford Dictionary of Nursery Rhymes*).

66 FOWER-AN-TWENTY HIELANDMEN. N. and W. Montgomerie, *Scottish Nursery Rhymes*, 1947.

66 LES TROIS LIMAÇONS. Claude Roy, *Trésor de la Poésie populaire*, 1954.

68 I PUT MY HAT UPON MY HEAD. Extempore parody of Thomas Percy's ballad 'The Hermit of Warkworth'.

68 AIKEN DRUM. Opie, *Oxford Dictionary of Nursery Rhymes*. The Opies mention a version in James Hogg's *Jacobite Relics*, 1821.

70 SONNET FOUND IN A DESERTED MAD-HOUSE. Carolyn Wells, *A Nonsense Anthology*, 1902.

70 HODDLEY, PODDLEY. *Oxford Dictionary of Nursery Rhymes*.

70 THREE YOUNG RATS. Rhys and Daglish, *The Land of Nursery Rhyme*, 1932. ? An American rhyme. *flats:* straw hats. *demi-veils:* half-length veils. *sorrel:* reddish brown.

71 from THE LOVES OF THE TRIANGLES, *The Poetry of the Anti-Jacobin*, 1799. Making fun of *The Loves of the Plants* by Erasmus Darwin, 1789.

72 from THE PROGRESS OF MAN. *The Poetry of the Anti-Jacobin*, 1799. Poking fun at *The Progress of Civil Society* by Richard Payne Knight, 1766.

73 SONG BY ROGERO. *The Poetry of the Anti-Jacobin*, 1799.

75 LUNAR STANZAS. Carolyn Wells, *A Nonsense Anthology*, 1902. From Knight's book *The Broken Harp*, 1815.

76 ONE OLD OX. Halliwell, *Nursery Rhymes of England*, 1853. *tee-totums:* four-sided gaming tops, each side with a letter indicating whether you take all or half or nothing, or stake again. *nonpareils:* tiny sugared almond sweets used for decorating puddings. In Flaubert's *Madame Bovary* the custards at the wedding feast were decorated with the initials of Charles and Emma 'in arabesques of nonpareils'.

76 THE DEAD PIG. F. W. Moorman, *Yorkshire Dialect Poems*, 1917. *lugs:* ears. *bed-flops:* leather swatters for killing vermin. *yune:* oven.

77 EAPER WEAPER. Norman Douglas, *London Street Games*, 1931.

77 THE OWL IN THE OAK. *Original Ditties for the Nursery*, 1807.

78 THE MUSES. W. T. Fernie, *Herbal Simples*, 1914.

78 NOTTAMUN TOWN. Cecil Sharp, *Nursery Songs from the Appalachian Mountains*.

79 OH, DEAR, WHAT CAN THE MATTER BE? Halliwell, *Nursery Rhymes of England*, 1853.

79 SHADRACH. Elizabeth Sewell, *The Field of Nonsense*, 1952. Shadrach, Meshach and Abed-nego, the three men thrown into the fiery furnace by Nebuchadnezzar, *Daniel* 3:19, 20.

79 MISTRESS TOWL. This and the next, two of the ancestral limericks, are from *The History of Sixteen Wonderful Old Women*, 1820.

80 THERE WAS AN OLD SOLDIER OF BICESTER. *Anecdotes and Adventures of Fifteen Gentlemen*, 1822, a booklet of limericks presumably by the same author as (above) *The History of Sixteen Wonderful Old Women*.

80 DAME WIGGINS. *Dame Wiggins of Lee and Her Seven Wonderful Cats. A Humorous Tale written principally by a Lady of Ninety*, 1823. Ruskin remembered it with gratitude and added some stanzas to a reprint in 1885. His version will be found in Vol. 2 of *The Works of John Ruskin*, ed. Cook and Wedderburn.

84 A CHILD THAT HAS A COLD. Thomas Dibdin's *Last Lays of the Last of the Three Dibdins* n.d.

84 THREE WISE MEN OF GOTHAM. *Mother Goose's Melody, c.* 1765. But the quatrain is earlier, no doubt. For the Gothamites see the longer poem and the note on it (pages 22 and 311).

84 THE WISE MEN OF GOTHAM. Thomas Love Peacock's *Paper Money Lyrics*, 1837. His poem goes on, another nine stanzas, to make fun of economists of the time, Paper Money Men as ready as any Gothamites 'to go to sea in a tub'. *S.T.C.:* Coleridge. *ΣΚΙΑΣ ONAP:* σκιᾶς ὄναρ

ἄνθρωπος, 'Man is a dream of a shadow', from Pindar's eighth Pythean Ode.

93 from MELODIES. Carroll's *Useful and Instructive Poetry*, ed. Derek Hudson, 1954. Written in 1845.

94 BROTHER AND SISTER. Date and source as above.

95 A VISITOR. As above.

95 MY FAIRY. As above.

96 A QUOTATION FROM SHAKESPEARE. As above.

100 THE PALACE OF HUMBUG. Carroll's *The Rectory Umbrella and Misch-Masch*, ed. Florence Milner, 1932.

103 ENTRANCE EXAMS. *The Adventures of Verdant Green*, 1853, by Cuthbert Bede, i.e. Edward Bradley.

104 POP GOES THE WEASEL. Victorian popular song of the 1850s. *the Eagle:* famous tavern in the City Road, London, which became an even more famous music hall. A sample perhaps of sense turning into acceptable nonsense because the meaning is lost—if it is true that the weasel was a hat-maker's block, in the East End trade, which the men would pawn or pop when out of work. Under *pop*, adverb, the Oxford Dictionary quotes 'Pop goes the Weasel' as the name of a new country dance in vogue in the 1850s. The dancers said 'Pop goes the weasel!' when each dancer darted under their arms to his partner.

105 AN EGGSTRAVAGANCE. Henry Ward Beecher (1813–87), brother of Harriet Beecher Stowe who wrote *Uncle Tom's Cabin*, was in his time America's most celebrated pulpit orator and moralist.

107 A LETTER TO EVELYN BARING. *Queery Leary Nonsense*, ed. Constance Strachey, 1911. Evelyn Baring, one of Lear's many eminent friends, statesman and 1st Earl of Cromer (1841–1917), nicknamed Overbaring.

107 SHE SITS UPON HER BULBUL. *Edward Lear*, Vivien Noakes, 1968. From his diary 4 April 1864.

109 THE COCK AND THE BULL. Nonsense in the mode of Browning.

113 HOW DOTH. Suggested by Isaac Watts's poem 'Against Idleness and Mischief' in *Divine Songs for the Use of Children*, 1715.

113 FATHER WILLIAM. Based on Southey's poem 'The Old Man's Comforts'.

114 THE MAD HATTER'S SONG. From Jane Taylor's poem 'The Star' in Jane and Anne Taylor's *Rhymes for the Nursery*, 1806.

117 THE DUCHESS'S LULLABY. Suggested by a popular poem beginning 'Speak gently; it is better far' (1849) by the American writer David Bates, Lewis Carroll relishing the second stanza:

> Speak gently to the little child;
> Its love be sure to gain;
> Teach it in accents soft and mild;
> It may not long remain.

117 ALICE'S RECITATION. Suggested by 'The Sluggard' in Isaac Watts's *Divine Songs for the Use of Children*, 1715.

118 TURTLE SOUP. From the popular song 'Star of the Evening' by J. M. Sayles, which Carroll heard the Liddell children sing in 1862 (*Diaries of Lewis Carroll*, ed. R. L. Greene, 1953).

119 THE MOCK TURTLE'S SONG. Suggested by Mary Howitt's moral tale in verse, 'The Spider and the Fly', in her *Sketches of Natural History*, 1834.

120 ECLOGUE. *Mr. Symonds:* the writer John Addington Symonds (1840–93).

124 THE CANNIBALS' GRACE. From Dickens's *Holiday Romance*, 1868.

125 FOREIGN LITERATURE. Thackeray published this piece of nonsense language in 1833 in the *National Standard*, which he edited.

126 A 'PRIZE' POEM. Shirley Brooks's *Wit and Humour*, 1875. Brooks (1816–74) was editor of *Punch*.

130 TÈMA CON VARIAZIÒNI. Tom Moore in his *Lalla Rookh* (in the part called 'The Fire-worshippers', 283) wrote

> I never nurs'd a dear gazelle,
>   To glad me with its soft black eye,
> But when it came to know me well.
> And love me, it was sure to die!

Irresistible. It stuck as well in the mind of Tom Hood the Younger (see 'A Few Muddled Metaphors', p. 142) and it lodged itself in Dickens: 'I never nursed a dear Gazelle, to glad me with its soft black eye, but when it came to know me well, and love me, it was sure to marry a market-gardener.'—*The Old Curiosity Shop*.

132 THE WHITE KNIGHT'S BALLAD. cf. the old man who gathered leeches in Wordsworth's 'Resolution and Independence'.

135 HUMPTY DUMPTY'S RECITATION. For Carroll's first line see the several Robin Hood ballads which begin 'In summer time when leaves grow green'.

137 THE WASP'S SONG. From Carroll's *The Wasp and the Wig*, ed. Martin Gardner, 1977.

138 THE WALRUS AND THE CARPENTER. For the movement cf. Thomas Hood's 'Dream of Eugene Aram'.

141 A QUADRUPEDREMIAN SONG. From Thomas Hood the Younger's *From Nowhere to the North Pole*, 1875.

142 SUNSET IN THE SEA. From 'Praeraphaelite Rhymes to a Picture of my native Sea-port' in Thomas Hood the Younger's *Quips and Cranks*, 1861.

142 A FEW MUDDLED METAPHORS. Thomas Hood the Younger's *Favourite Poems*, 1877. For the dear gazelle see note above on Lewis Carroll's 'Tèma con variaziòni'.

143 HOW SINGULAR. ibid.

143 CONFOUNDED NONSENSE. From *Fun* (which Thomas Hood the Younger edited), 11 August 1866.

144 SHE LOST HER SHEEP. *Tom Hood's Comic Annual* for 1873.

144 FOUR AND TWENTY MERULAE. ibid.

145 THE FIR-TREE OF BOSNIA. *The Book of Nonsense*, ed. R. L. Green, 1956.

146 from VERS NONSENSIQUES. George du Maurier, *A Legend of Camelot. Pictures and Poems*, 1898. *Cassez, cassez, cassez* in the first limerick, travestying Tennyson's *Break, Break, Break*.

152 MENU. Robert Congreve's preface to *Later Letters of Edward Lear*, ed. Constance Strachey, 1911.

157 COLD ARE THE CRABS. Lear's *Teapots and Quails*, ed. Angus Davidson and Philip Hofer, 1953.

158 SCRAPS OF LEAR. 1, 2, 4 are from *Later Letters of Edward Lear*, ed. Constance Strachey, 1911 (31 October 1881, 1 January 1870, 13 February 1860). 3 comes from *Letters of Edward Lear*, ed. Constance Strachey, 1907.

158 AFTER TENNYSON. MS. letter, 12 September 1873, to Chichester Fortescue, Somerset Record Office, Taunton; and *Later Letters of Edward Lear*, ed. Constance Strachey, 1911. Lear had made drawings illustrating the original lines in Tennyson (in 'The Lotos-Eaters').

159 MORE SCRAPS OF LEAR. *Later Letters of Edward Lear*, ed. Constance Strachey, 1911. 1, 31 January 1885; 2, 16 April 1884; 3, 19 February 1886.

163 FERDINANDO AND ELVIRA. *Poet Close*: John Close (1816–91), doggerel writer of Kirkby Stephen, celebrated for award and withdrawal of civil list pension.

167 THE CHILDREN OF THE OWL AND THE PUSSY-CAT. *Edward Lear*, Angus Davidson, 1938.

168 RIDDLES. *Later Letters of Edward Lear*, ed. Constance Strachey, 1911.

173 MRS JAYPHER. *Queery Leary Nonsense*, ed. Constance Strachey, 1911. Edward Lear's instruction was that this should be read 'sententiously and with grave importance'.

173 MRS JAYPHER ON LEMONS. ibid.

173 DINGLE BANK. From *Queery Leary Nonsense*, ed. Constance Strachey, 1911.

198 MORE LIMERICKS. 1, 2, 3, 5, from Edward Lear, *Teapots and Quails*, ed. Angus Davidson and Philip Hofer, 1953. 4, from Osgood Field's *Lear on my Shelves*, New York, 1933.

212 TUTOR'S DIGNITY. From a letter in *The Lewis Carroll Picture Book*, ed. S. D. Collingwood, 1899.

213 SYZYGY CHAINS. The first is from *The Life and Letters of Lewis Carroll*, ed. S. D. Collingwood, 1898. The second is an example from Carroll's *Syzygies and Lanrick*, 1893. Carroll invented his game of syzygies (syzygy, Greek συζυγία, a conjunction or yoking) in 1879.

213 HIT OR MISS. A selection of the ninety-one pairs of premisses in chap. 4, 'Hit or Miss', in Carroll's *The Game of Logic*, 1887.

214 LIONS AND GRUEL AND UNCLES. From Carroll's *The Game of Logic*, 1887.

215 FRAGMENT OF A SONG. From 'The Legend of Scotland' in *The Lewis Carroll Picture Book*, ed. S. D. Collingwood, 1899.

216 THE LITTLE MAN THAT HAD A LITTLE GUN. A Swinburnian piece (cf. Swinburne's 'Dolores').

218 COME INTO THE ORCHARD, ANNE. Tennyson into Swinburne.

218 NEPHELIDIA. Swinburne making fun of Swinburne.

220 THE HIGHER PANTHEISM. Tennyson into Swinburne again.

221 SELECT SPOONERISMS. Though he was odd at times in speech, there is no evidence that W. A. Spooner, Dean and afterwards Warden of New College, Oxford, ever in fact uttered a spoonerism. But such word-nonsense fitted well into an Oxford used to the word-nonsense of that other Oxford don, Lewis Carroll (Spooner's dates were 1844–1930).

222 LITTLE BIRDS. This was written first as a separate poem. Then 'A Pig's Tale' was inserted—tale within tale—and the new composite poem was published in *Sylvie and Bruno Concluded*, 1893. For the additional stanza inserted, see *Diaries of Lewis Carroll*, ed. R. L. Green, 1953, vol. 2, p. 543.

226 THE PESSIMIST. *Ben King's Verses*, New York, 1894.

229 THE BOY OF QUEBEC. *Home Book of Verse for Young Folks*, ed. B. E. Stevenson, New York, 1929. His daughter vehemently denied the usual ascription of this to Rudyard Kipling.

229 A WOMAN'S REASON. From *The Burgess Nonsense Book*, 1914.

229 REMARKABLE ART. ibid.

230 TRAPPING FAIRIES. ibid.

230 A RADICAL CREED. ibid.

231 ON DRAWING-ROOM AMENITIES. ibid.

231 THE SHADES OF NIGHT. From *A.E.H.*, ed. Laurence Housman, 1937.

233 INFANT INNOCENCE. ibid.

234 G. K. CHESTERTON ON HIS BIRTH. ibid. These lines came to Housman in a dream.

234 AMELIA MIXED THE MUSTARD. ibid.

234 MR. ODY MET A BODY. *Westminster Gazette*, 21 June 1951, included by R. L. Green in his *Century of Humorous Verse 1850–1950*, 1959.

272 DID YOU EVER, EVER, EVER. *The American Song-bag*, ed. Carl Sandburg, 1927.

274 MY MAMMY WAS A WALL-EYED GOAT. *American Tramp and Underworld Slang*, ed. Godfrey Irwin, 1931.

274 I SCREAM. Treasury of American Folklore, ed. B. A. Botkin, 1944.

274 BESTIAIRE SANS PRÉNOM. From Hans Arp's *Le Siège de l'air, poèmes*, 1915–45.

276 I AM A HORSE. *Three Painter Poets*, tr. Harriet Watts, 1974.

277 TWO LITTLE ARABS ADULT AND ARABESQUE. ibid.

279 WHEN IT BURNS BEFORE THE HARPS. ibid.

279 THE DYING AIRMAN. A slightly different version in *The Oxford Book of Light Verse*, ed. W. H. Auden, 1938.

280 AN ANGLICAN CURATE IN WANT. R. A. Knox, *In Three Tongues*, 1959.

280 PICNIC RHYME. B. A. Botkin, *A Treasury of American Folklore*, 1944.

284 LIMERICKS. Conrad Aiken, *A Seizure of Limericks*, 1965.

285 AWAKE, MY LUTE. *Atlantic Monthly*, November 1943. N.S.—i.e. *non satis*, not enough, the marking for a failure.

286 LA SARDINE. Robert Desnos, *Chantefables et Chantefleurs*, 1944.

287 LA COLOMBE DE L'ARCHE. Robert Desnos, *Corps et biens*, 1953.

287 LE PÉLICAN. Robert Desnos, *Chantefables et Chantefleurs*, 1944.

288 LE GÉRANIUM. ibid.

288 LE LAMA. ibid.

324

288 LES HIBOUX. ibid.

289 LE KANGOUROU. ibid.

292 THE COMMON CORMORANT. Christopher Isherwood, *Exhumations*, 1966.

293 LES PONTS S'EFFONDRENT TOUS. From 'Blanc Seing' in *Corps et biens*, 1953.

294 ISABELLE ET MARIE. Robert Desnos, *Corps et biens*, 1953.

296 A SONNET. *Russia's Lost Literature of the Absurd*, ed. George Gibian, 1971.

297 VINDICATION. ibid.

298 THE CONNECTION. ibid.

300 THE WITCH'S WORK SONG. T. H. White, *The Sword in the Stone*, 1938.

Index of Writers, Poems and Prose

331

335

Index of First Lines and Titles

343

348